ⓓECORATIVE
MACHINE STITCHERY

DECORATIVE MACHINE STITCHERY

design, techniques and projects
for every sewing machine

BY ROBBIE FANNING

illustrations and photos
by Tony and Robbie Fanning

Butterick Publishing

for my parents, Pat and Roberta Losey Patterson

Library of Congress Catalog Card Number: 76-4396
International Standard Book Number: 0-88421-050-2
Copyright © 1976 by Butterick Publishing
161 Sixth Avenue, New York, New York 10013
A Division of American Can Company

COVER STITCHERY BY ROBBIE FANNING
COVER DESIGN BY JEFF BOYLE
BOOK DESIGN BY BETTY BINNS

PRINTED IN U.S.A.

CONTENTS

ACKNOWLEDGEMENTS

Thanks first to Don Douglas of Douglas Fabrics
(Palo Alto, California) for sharing so much so freely;
second, to my special friends, family and otherwise,
for their support; third, to my editor, Evelyn
Brannon, and my agent, Elyse Sommer; and most
important, to our daughter, Kali Koala, for
consistently telling friends that her mother is a
writer and an artist.

PREFACE:

The woodworker has a lathe; the potter has a wheel; and I have my sewing machine. This is my tool, my vehicle for expressing a lifelong love of fabric and thread.

Because there are so many exciting machine stitchery techniques, each has been isolated into a chapter, showing you first the possible effects and then presenting an immediately usable example that draws on your new knowledge. In this way, each chapter builds on the previous ones and each project serves as a learn-by-doing sampler of techniques. I want you to be able to sail off on your own projects with a minimum of back-sliding and frustration, so I've written in the minor pit-falls of each technique.

I've also described my way of working the projects in great detail, more to help you understand the process and order of working machine stitchery than to serve as a guide to be slavishly copied. Just as the patterns at the fabric store are merely a take-off point for our own choices of color and fabric, these designs are meant to be changed to fit your viewpoint. In fact, one of the joys of machine stitchery is its variety and spontaneity. Give ten machine stitchers the same design and the results will be wonderfully different, according to what threads were used top and bottom, which tensions selected, what background fabric chosen, even how fast or slow the machine stitched.

To further motivate your own work, there is a gallery section of artists working in the medium, with some specific information on how they achieved their results.

And you *don't* have to own a fancy machine that does 400 stitches and walks the dog to do most of the designs in this book. Even the zigzag work can be done on a treadle machine, although obviously it's much more laborious. My hope is that through this book, you will learn the capabilities of your machine and then be able to combine what you've learned with the sense of fun, discovery, and inspiration that we all feel towards our craft.

Robbie Fanning
Menlo Park, California

ONE

INTRODUCING DECORATIVE MACHINE STITCHERY

Aside from being beautiful, unique, and sensuous, decorative machine stitchery has one overwhelming factor in its favor: it's fast. Nothing is quite as satisfying as envisioning a colorful, heavily embroidered garment and then actually being able to complete it in one afternoon. With machine embroidery, large areas of texture and color can be filled in a short time. Ideas can be executed before inspiration fades.

And the scope of possible effects done on a machine is staggering. Say that you had eight distinct settings for stitch length, going from the tightest stitch to the loosest basting stitch. And say that your zigzag machine had five settings from 0 (or no zigzag) to a wide zigzag. Add to those the various tension settings of upper and bobbin threads and throw in a few thousand variations in color and texture of threads. While you're at it, consider various needle sizes and the million types of fabrics available to us. Feed it to a mathematician and (s)he'll tell you that there are at least 80 septillion (80,000,000,000,000,000,000,000,000) possible combinations. And that's for a single stitch! (Diagram 1)

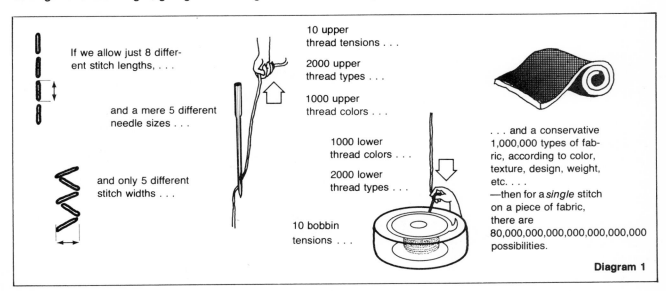

If we allow just 8 different stitch lengths, . . .

and a mere 5 different needle sizes . . .

and only 5 different stitch widths . . .

10 upper thread tensions . . .

2000 upper thread types . . .

1000 upper thread colors . . .

1000 lower thread colors . . .

2000 lower thread types . . .

10 bobbin tensions . . .

. . . and a conservative 1,000,000 types of fabric, according to color, texture, design, weight, etc. . . .
—then for a *single* stitch on a piece of fabric, there are 80,000,000,000,000,000,000,000,000 possibilities.

Diagram 1

Plate 1
From the center out: eyelet, free machine embroidery from the underside with a heavy thread in the bobbin, automatic stitch, free machine whip stitch, satin stitch with extra-fine rayon thread, free machine on top-side with hoop, automatic stitch, cut work on net, couching-by-piercing

Here are but a few of the 80 septillion. The specific how-to's of each technique are in the chapter texts. (Plate 1)

How difficult is machine embroidery? If I can hold a four-year-old on my lap and merely run the foot pedal for her as she free machine embroiders, you can do it too.

You don't need a fancy zigzag machine to do most of the work in these chapters, except for the specific sections on decorative cams and zigzag. On the other hand, if you're thinking of buying a machine, I would recommend buying one that does have a zigzag because it increases the versatility of your work. Besides the extension of decorative possibilities, you can then handle all kinds of knit fabrics, from the lightest tricot to the heavy sweater knits, including both garment construction and embellishment.

No matter what your make of machine, though, learn how to take care of it by reading its instruction manual and by consulting a reputable sewing machine dealer. A book such as this can hardly touch the wealth of knowledge that a helpful dealer with years of experience has. For example, my machine has a rotary bobbin case that travels twice as far for each stitch as the rest of the machine; therefore it is vitally important that I keep my bobbin shuttle hook well-oiled. I oil my machine before every major project and if it doesn't seem to sew as quietly as usual, I oil that hook more often. (I also sing to my machine as I work, figuring that if it works on plants, it might work on machines too.)

Dust and lint are the enemies of your machine. Clean its innards every time you sit down to sew. About every eighteen months, either take the machine apart yourself for a thorough vacuuming and cleaning out of gunk, or take it to a dealer. We don't think twice about taking a car in for a periodic tune-up; why not treat your sewing machine with the same respect? With proper care, a good machine can last a lifetime.

Because there is no standard language for machine embroidery, you and I may use different terms for the same part of a machine. Therefore, here is a picture of a sewing machine, labelled with the terms I use (Diagram 2). Your machine may differ—see your own instruction manual. I will also start each chapter with a pictorial glossary of the terms used therein.

What supplies will you need for machine stitchery? Obviously a machine. You will also need a supply of machine needles in the various sizes. Incidentally, buy

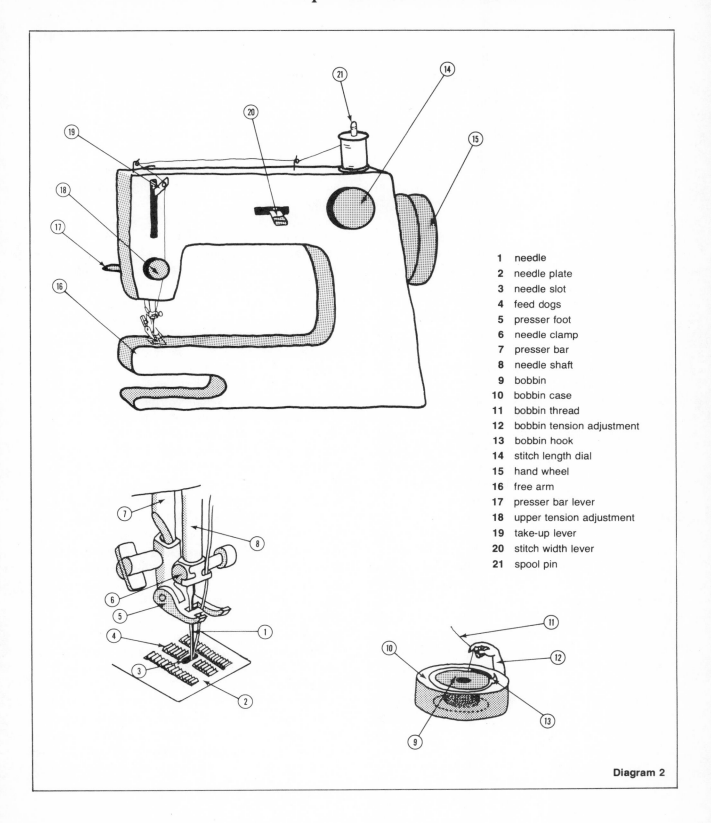

1   needle
2   needle plate
3   needle slot
4   feed dogs
5   presser foot
6   needle clamp
7   presser bar
8   needle shaft
9   bobbin
10   bobbin case
11   bobbin thread
12   bobbin tension adjustment
13   bobbin hook
14   stitch length dial
15   hand wheel
16   free arm
17   presser bar lever
18   upper tension adjustment
19   take-up lever
20   stitch width lever
21   spool pin

Diagram 2

the needles made for your machine instead of grabbing the nearest packet at the fabric store. One reason the machine may be skipping stitches is that you're using a needle not suited to your machine. Specific needles for specific threads and fabrics will be discussed in Chapter 2, but in general, fit the thread to the type of work or material, and fit the needle to the thread. But even the best machine will give shoddy results with a bad needle. If you sew over a lot of pins or have been using the same needle for years, put in a new needle for your machine embroidery projects.

Thread is not so expensive that you cannot afford to treat yourself to one spool in at least all the rainbow colors. (Remember ROY G. BIV? Red/orange/yellow /green/blue/indigo/violet.) And while you're buying, throw in a few extra bobbins. The nicest present I've given myself recently is ten new bobbins.

What threads are appropriate for machine stitchery? Believe it or not, almost any, from the finest embroidery thread to four-ply wool. Some of the thick slubby threads cannot be threaded through a needle and should be wound onto the bobbin and stitched in a special way (see Chapter 6), or laid on the surface and couched down, but any thread that inspires you can probably be incorporated into your work. However, the greater part of your machine embroidery will be done with 100% cotton thread, so buy a decent supply of it.

Since twenty percent of the weight of cotton threads is water, after the thread sits around for awhile, it dries out, becomes brittle, and breaks when you sew. Either leave the thread outside overnight so dew will soak into the thread (but bring it in before the sun dries it out again), or store it in the refrigerator with the leftovers.

As for appropriate machine embroidery fabrics, anything a needle will pass through is fair game, from gauze to leather. Some possibilities come to mind immediately, like cotton fabrics for appliqué. But beautiful machine stitchery is done on see-through plastic, organza, felt, and a host of other unusual fabrics—see Chapters 9-12.

Other supplies you will need are the regular sewing supplies, such as sharp scissors, pins, tissue paper, and tape measure, as well as some from the desk drawer—graph paper, ruler, felt-tip pen. I also keep a pair of tweezers near the machine for pulling out small pieces of typing paper from the back of machine-embroidered garments, and for extracting lint and broken threads from the bobbin case. A needle threader is helpful, too, for guiding thicker threads like buttonhole twist through the machine needle. (Plate 2)

You will also use a 6″(15cm) or 8″(20,5cm) embroidery hoop quite often and may want to wrap its inside ring, the one without the screw or hinge on it, with strips of cotton fabric or bias tape. When you stretch material in the hoop, particularly the lightweight fabrics like organza, cotton strips keep the fabric from slipping and puckering—more on this in Chapter 4.

One other thing you will need is not really a supply, but it will greatly increase your chances of success in machine embroidery. For every project, set up a small (say, 3″[7,5cm] X 6″[15cm]) rectangle of the very same fabric you're sewing on, to be used as a doodle cloth. On this cloth practice the stitches you intend to use in your stitchery. If the stitches pucker the fabric of your doodle cloth, loosen the upper and lower tensions until you reach a desirable result, always keeping track of your changes by writing directly on the doodle cloth with a felt-tip pen. When you find the best tension settings and the best thread variation for your work, you will know how to proceed on the actual item to be embroidered. And if you save this doodle cloth, pinning it to your pattern or filing it in a sewing drawer, you will always be able to duplicate your efforts with a minimum of initial experimenting. (Plate 3)

Another factor will improve your efforts one hundred percent: an iron. Mother was right; pressing makes the difference between sloppiness and craftsmanship.

Now you know what's possible with machine stitchery: it's not too difficult for you and your machine, and the supplies won't deplete your bank account. Next you need to find out how to transfer a design from a piece of paper to your fabric.

Many times you will want to enlarge a small design into something bigger or reduce one from something larger, so it is useful to know how to blow up a design. Fortunately there is a technique which lets you do this, even if you can't draw for beans. Most of the patterns in this book are reproduced full-size, but those that are reduced have a helpful ¼″(6mm) grid printed over them. On your own, you can achieve the same effect

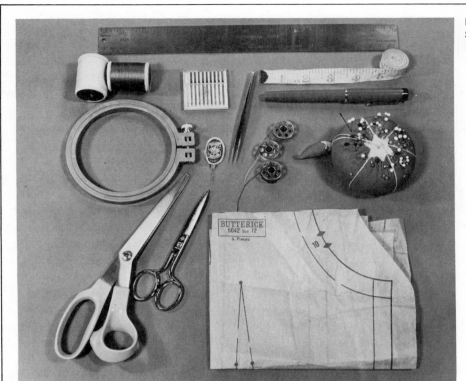

Plate 2
Supplies for Machine
Embroidery

Plate 3
Typical Doodle Cloth

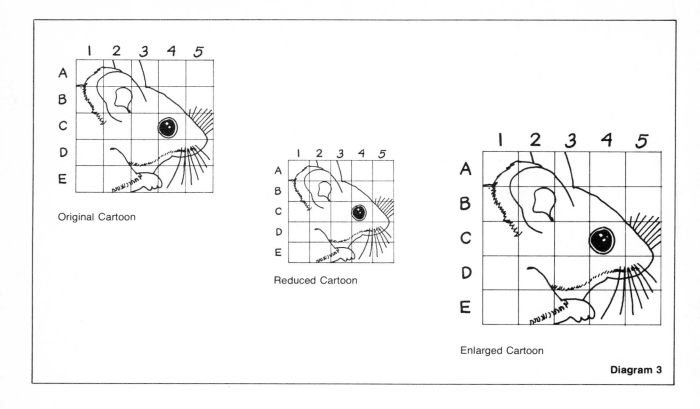

Original Cartoon

Reduced Cartoon

Enlarged Cartoon

Diagram 3

by laying ¼ "(6mm) graph paper over a design and tracing the design onto it. Decide how much bigger you want the design—twice the size?, three times? Number and letter the squares as shown. Now take a fresh sheet of ¼ "(6mm) graph paper and a ruler and rule off new squares. For example, if you want your new design twice as big, rule off every other line, both horizontally and vertically. If you want your finished design three times the size, rule off every third line. You will now have squares which are twice or three times the size of your original squares. Number and letter these new squares in exactly the same order as you did the original design. Start with square 1A and draw in the larger square whatever you see in the smaller square. Do this for each square . . . and surprise!, your design is enlarged.

Now you can use one of the seven transfer methods to place your design onto the material you've chosen. (Diagram 3)

There are at least seven good methods to transfer designs onto fabric for machine embroidery, each de-

pendent on the kind of fabric you've chosen. These methods work when the design is already the exact size you want. Then you can use one of the seven methods to transfer your design to your material.

Before we delve into the ways you can transfer designs to your material, we should decide how much of the design to transfer. Here, as is often the case, the rule is "least is best." In general, only the main lines or curves of your design need to be sketched in. At best, only the outlines of large, filled-in areas need to be put onto the transferred design.

The old, venerable name for such a line drawing is "cartoon." Long before the Saturday morning TV cartoons, the great painters of the Italian Renaissance were using cartoons to put their preliminary sketches for frescoes upon walls. We'll bow to tradition, even though the name "cartoon" now has an added connotation of fun . . . come to think of it, even the more modern use of "cartoon" fits what we're doing. (Diagram 4)

In the remainder of this book, whenever we talk

about the design you're working, we'll assume that you can reduce your design to cartoon form. In particular, when you want to transfer your design to fabric, you'll want to imagine the "center line" your needle will follow as you stitch—this will define your cartoon for you.

The cartoons at the end of each chapter show the direction you're stitching, in addition to the center line. This becomes especially important when you're using decorative cams with directional designs. If you own this book, make copious notes on the colors to use, types of stitches, etc., directly on the cartoon. Prop up the book as you work on the machine.

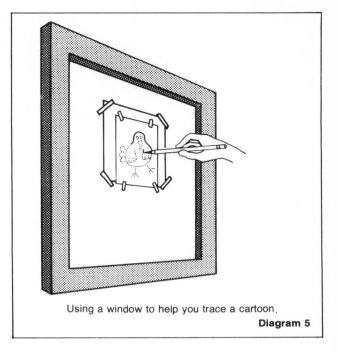

Using a window to help you trace a cartoon.

Diagram 5

Reduce complicated pictures to cartoon form for stitching.

Diagram 4

Onward, to methods of transferring designs—my favorite is to lay a piece of tracing or tissue paper over the cartoon and to copy it with a black felt-tip pen. I often use the wrong side of outdated or extra tissue paper from clothing patterns, ignoring any print on the tissue. Wait a minute for the ink of the felt-tip pen to dry, so it won't smudge your fabric, then tape the tissue paper to a window (during the day—what you're doing is making a make-shift light table). Tape the fabric over the tissue, centering the design, and trace the design onto the fabric with pencil or tailor's chalk. Caution: If you know the design line will not be completely covered by the sewing machine thread, don't use an ordinary pencil for tracing the design as it does not always wash out. You could also use a fine brush and blue watercolor, taking care not to mix too runny a mixture. On dark material I use a white pencil and on light material, a blue one. This method of tracing works on a surprising number of fabrics—from the most transparent fabric through medium-weight cottons with even surfaces. It does not work well on linen and other textured fabrics. (Diagram 5)

Another way to transfer designs that is particularly suited to the machine is to copy the cartoon onto a

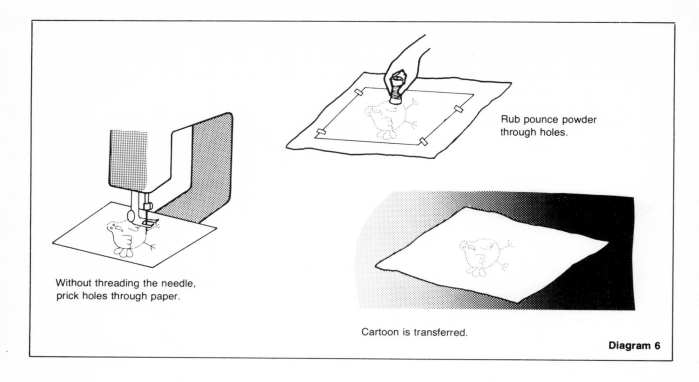

Without threading the needle, prick holes through paper.

Rub pounce powder through holes.

Cartoon is transferred.

Diagram 6

piece of typing paper and then to sew along the lines with an unthreaded machine, using a Size 9 (60) sewing machine needle so that the holes in the paper are not too big. Pin or cello-tape the paper to your fabric, centering the design wherever you want it, and gently rub pounce powder (similar to resin powder and available from needlework stores, or see Supply List) over the line of holes. I use a rolled-up pad of felt to apply the pounce to the fabric, gently rolling it into the holes of the typing paper and taking care not to put too much charcoal onto the design at once. Pull up one corner of the typing paper from time to time to check whether enough pounce has gone through the holes to mark your design sufficiently. Then carefully lift off the taped paper and lightly blow off the surplus pounce. If you try to brush it off, the pounce will smudge the fabric. This method works well on all fabric except the heavily textured and is especially useful for transferring repeat patterns. (Diagram 6)

Since we often put a backing of organza or batiste on fabric before machine stitching, a third method of transferring designs becomes quite easy. Put the or-

ganza (white is easiest to work with) directly over the cartoon and trace with a dark line. If the item being machine-stitched will ever be washed, use only felt-tip pens that are guaranteed waterproof (such as canvas work or needlepoint markers). You can use a pencil in this case, since the organza will be on the back of the fabric. Now machine-baste the organza to the back of your fabric, with the design *against* the wrong side of the fabric; otherwise you'll have a mirror image on the topside. Because you're using white organza, the design will show through to the underside of the organza. Load your bobbin with a thread that is slightly lighter or darker than the color of your fabric. Baste the design, the organza facing up and the topside of the fabric against the needle plate. You now have transferred the design to the right side, where it is marked by your bobbin thread. A variation of this method is to trace the design or draw directly onto iron-on interfacing, which is then bonded to the back of your fabric. However, the design will be a mirror image on the right side, of course, when you machine-baste through the interfacing. (Diagram 7)

To transfer a design with dressmaker's carbon paper, available in any fabric store, tape your fabric to a hard surface, like a glass-topped desk or a Formica kitchen counter. Trace the cartoon onto tissue or tracing paper and center it on the fabric, weighing down the top edge with anything handy and heavy (scissors, paper weights, clean flower pots). Carefully slip a piece of dressmaker's carbon paper—don't use typing carbon paper because it smudges—between the tracing and the fabric, and then anchor the bottom edges of the tracing paper over it. Trace the design with an empty ball-point pen or the handle end of a letter opener. You have to push hard to produce a decent line on the fabric, but not so hard as to tear the tissue paper. (Diagram 8)

Transfer pencils are now available in needlework

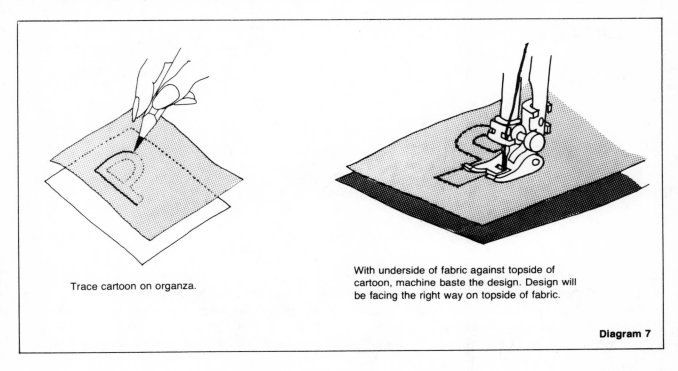

Trace cartoon on organza.

With underside of fabric against topside of cartoon, machine baste the design. Design will be facing the right way on topside of fabric.

Diagram 7

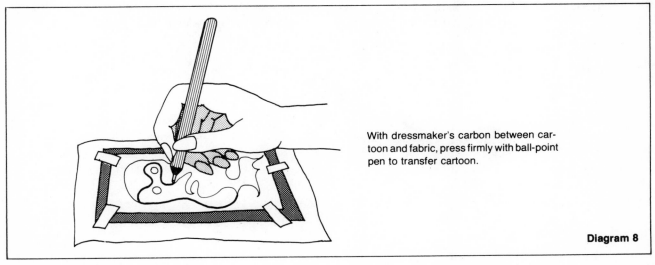

With dressmaker's carbon between cartoon and fabric, press firmly with ball-point pen to transfer cartoon.

Diagram 8

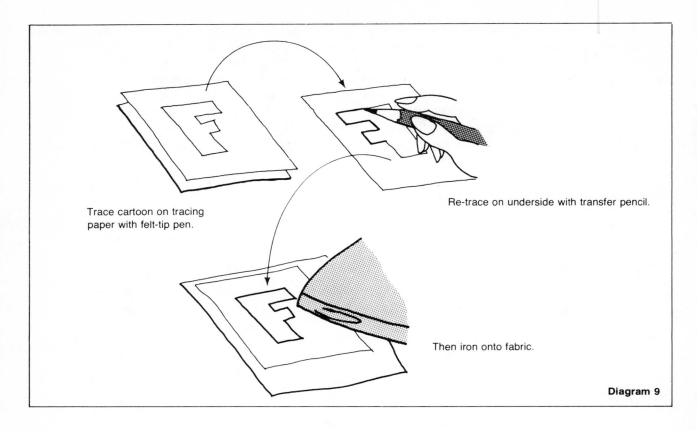

Trace cartoon on tracing paper with felt-tip pen.

Re-trace on underside with transfer pencil.

Then iron onto fabric.

Diagram 9

stores (see Supply List), taking some of the fuss out of transferring the design. Lay the tissue or tracing paper over the cartoon and copy with a felt-tip pen. Let the ink dry and then turn the tissue paper over and retrace the design on the wrong side with the transfer pencil. Now lay the tissue paper on top of the fabric, the transfer pencil side against the fabric, and pin it carefully in place. Use an iron as hot as your fabric permits. Since the transfer lines sometimes rub off later as you work, as soon as the transfer cools, I like to machine-baste the main lines of the design as a safety precaution. (Diagram 9)

Transferring a design to heavily textured fabric can be a problem. Transfer pencil, pounce, and carbon

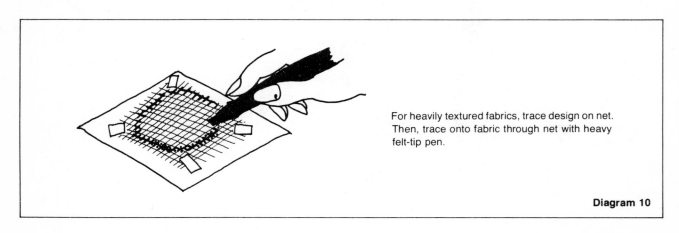

For heavily textured fabrics, trace design on net. Then, trace onto fabric through net with heavy felt-tip pen.

Diagram 10

lines are lost in the bumps of the fabric and even machine basting lines can be difficult to follow. Occasionally I lay white net over the cartoon and copy the design with a felt-tip pen (if you're copying from a library book, lay a protective piece of tissue paper over the design and don't use a felt-tip pen as it will bleed through the tissue paper—use a crayon instead). Then I lay the net over the fabric and retrace the design lines with a fat-tipped felt-tip pen (waterproof), which runs through the holes of the net onto the fabric. This isn't my favorite method as the results are vague and wavery, but sometimes this is the only method that works. (Diagram 10)

The other method I use on heavily textured fabric is to cut the main design shapes out of paper (typing or construction), pin the papers to the fabric, and machine-baste around the outsides of the paper, not catching the edges. I then remove the pins and cut up the construction paper into little bits, placing them inside letters to my mother so that when she opens the envelope, a shower of confetti brightens her day. (Diagram 11)

It's important to use matching fabrics in machine embroidery. I once sent a friend a zigzag message on felt, which she decided would make a great patch for her jeans. Felt is not washable, which she forgot until her first trip to the laundromat.

Threads, too, must be carefully chosen for washability. I heard a sad story about a white polyester knit dress with red silk floss topstitching, made for a prestigious fashion show. It was handled and soiled so much before the show that someone tossed it into the washing machine. Those pitiful pink streaks never did come out.

Preshrink your fabric, straighten the grain, test it for colorfastness—all those boring preliminaries prevent

Do's . . .

- ▦ fit the thread to the type of work or material and fit the needle to the thread
- ▦ read your machine's instruction manual
- ▦ keep your machine well-oiled and lint-free
- ▦ treat yourself to a rainbow of thread colors and extra bobbins
- ▦ use a doodle cloth and an iron
- ▦ match fabrics and thread to ultimate use
- ▦ experiment to find the best way of working on your machine

AND DON'TS

- ▦ stand on your machine or run over your fingers
- ▦ force machine—it will do the job better and safer at the speed at which it was designed
- ▦ run over pins or use a blunt or bent needle
- ▦ let your cotton thread dry out
- ▦ use a pencil to transfer designs when the pencil line may not be completely covered by the stitching

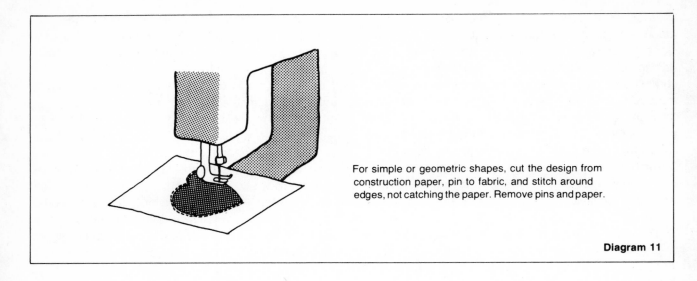

For simple or geometric shapes, cut the design from construction paper, pin to fabric, and stitch around edges, not catching the paper. Remove pins and paper.

Diagram 11

that gut-wrenching feeling of spending hours on a garment that is ruined by the first wash.

Also, when working on a garment, don't cut out the exact pattern shape before machine embroidering. Do the work and then cut out the pattern piece, to prevent unalterable puckering.

Although machine stitchery has its own visual identity and should not be an attempt to imitate handwork, it does combine beautifully with all kinds of hand embroidery—stitchery, patchwork, drawn thread, and many more. If this book touches you at all, by the last chapter you will be eager to further develop your own ideas. Therefore I would like to stress that there is never only one way to do any of the techniques and procedures herein. Experiment on your machine and find the way that works best for you.

TWO

STRAIGHT STITCH

GLOSSARY

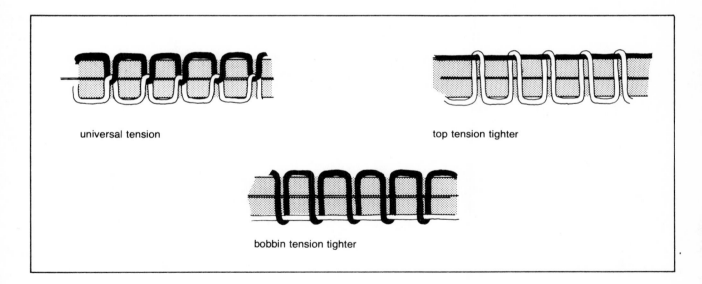

universal tension

top tension tighter

bobbin tension tighter

THE TECHNIQUE

Even if you did nothing but straight stitch machine embroidery, you would have enough ideas and work to keep you busy the rest of your life—that's how versatile this simple stitch is.

Straight stitch is often used to outline a shape, at the same time securing it to a background, as in appliqué. It is also used to emphasize a line with a thicker thread, such as the use of buttonhole twist in topstitching.

A lovely decorative effect can be had quickly and easily by combining rows of running stitch with hand embroidery. (Plate 4)

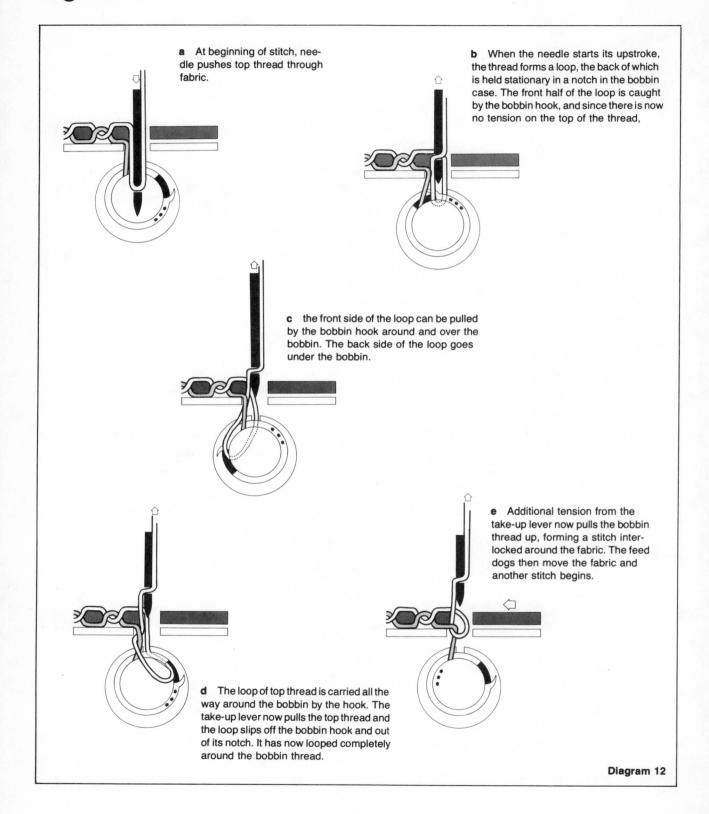

a At beginning of stitch, needle pushes top thread through fabric.

b When the needle starts its upstroke, the thread forms a loop, the back of which is held stationary in a notch in the bobbin case. The front half of the loop is caught by the bobbin hook, and since there is now no tension on the top of the thread,

c the front side of the loop can be pulled by the bobbin hook around and over the bobbin. The back side of the loop goes under the bobbin.

e Additional tension from the take-up lever now pulls the bobbin thread up, forming a stitch interlocked around the fabric. The feed dogs then move the fabric and another stitch begins.

d The loop of top thread is carried all the way around the bobbin by the hook. The take-up lever now pulls the top thread and the loop slips off the bobbin hook and out of its notch. It has now looped completely around the bobbin thread.

Diagram 12

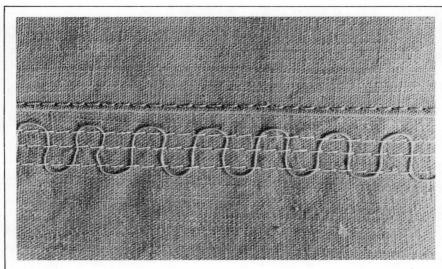

Plate 4 From the top down: appliqué with buttonhole twist, rows of straight stitch embellished with hand embroidery

But before going any further, let me ask you an embarrassing question: Do you really know how a stitch is formed on the sewing machine?

Don't laugh—understanding how the machine works explains how it doesn't. And don't be embarrassed—in a continuing private survey, I've discovered that most people do not understand how a stitch is formed, even if they have been sewing on a machine all their lives. (Diagram 12)

Now you can see that if, for example, the fabric is not flat against the needle plate at the moment the needle enters the fabric, the shuttle hook on the bobbin will not catch the loop of top thread, and therefore a stitch will be skipped. Later, when you are doing free machine embroidery, remember this information. (Diagram 13)

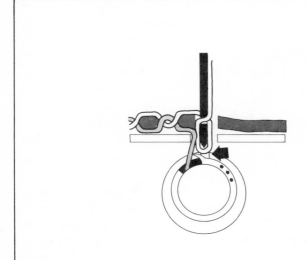

If the fabric is not held against the needle plate, the bobbin hook can miss the loop of top thread, and a stitch is dropped.

Diagram 13

Some of the other bugaboos you might run into, and why they occur, are:

1 The upper thread breaks:

  a the machine is not threaded properly or the needle is inserted wrong way round or at the wrong height;

  b upper tension is too tight;

  c the thread is dry and brittle; or too thick for either the needle or material; or knotted somewhere between the top spool and the needle;

  d the needle is bent or blunt;

  e the presser foot is not lowered.

2 The lower thread breaks:

  a lower tension is too tight;

  b the thread is unevenly wound on the bobbin or brought up incorrectly;

  c the hole in the needle plate is old and scarred and needs a light filing with a machinist's file (**sewing machine dealer** can do this).

3 The needle breaks:

  a the material has been jerked during sewing, bending the needle and causing it to hit the presser foot or needle plate;

  b the upper tension is too tight for the machine;

  c the needle is mounted incorrectly.

4 Stitches are uneven or skipped:

  a the bobbin innards are linty and clogged;

  b needles being used are not made expressly for machine;

  c the machine is incorrectly threaded;

  d the fabric was not touching the needle plate at the **moment the stitch was formed.**

5 The material puckers:

  a thread is too thick for material;

  b upper and/or lower tensions are too tight;

  c stitches are too long,

  d fabric was jerked away from needle at end of stitching, gathering fabric, rather than pulling gently to side, pinching ends of threads;

  e fabric needs added body to withstand heavy stitching.

Any other irregularities, such as poor timing or a sluggish machine, should be checked by a dealer.

I won't fill your ear with the details of which needle and thread to use with which fabric. If I start listing them here, you'll just yawn and say "Oh that" and you won't learn anything at all. So right now I'll tell you the barest minimum and when in the future you need some hardcore information, you can turn to the Needle and Thread Chart on page 190. Incidentally, American, Japanese, and European needles have different numbering systems, which is why I always give two numbers.

Most of your machine stitchery will be done with 100% cotton sewing machine thread. At the moment, most fabric stores carry only Size 50, a number that refers to the thickness of the thread. Don't ask me why, but the fatter the thread, the smaller the number. Therefore, buttonhole twist, which is thicker than ordinary sewing machine thread, is Size 30. It's doubly confusing because an American Size 50 thread is thicker than a European Size 50. To avoid confusion, I will describe threads as extra-fine, ordinary, and heavy, rather than refer to a size number.

I use cotton-covered polyester for garment construction, but hardly at all for machine stitchery as the outer fiber tends to shred, causing the thread to knot and break. However, since new threads are being introduced all the time, don't reject any thread without giving it a thorough workout. For example, there is a new cotton-covered polyester, much finer in thickness, that handles beautifully.

We are now beginning to see in fabric stores European and Asian threads of 100% cotton, 100% rayon, and 100% polyester which are extra-fine and produce, in particular, stunning free machine embroidery.

Check the Supply List for sources and ask your favorite fabric store to stock a full range of colors.

In most cases you will use a Size 12 (80) needle with ordinary sewing machine thread, but remember that you choose the thread to suit the fabric and the needle to suit the thread. On organza, for example, you would choose a Size 10 (70) needle and extra-fine cotton sewing machine thread.

You're impatient to start sewing, aren't you? But before you can do even an inch of straight stitch, your fabric must be prepared. If your fabric will later be washed, preshrink it now by wetting the fabric and drying it in a hot dryer (except for permanent press fabrics—use a cool to warm dryer). If you're making something that will be washed, be sure your threads are colorfast (silk floss, for example, is not guaranteed colorfast).

Some fabrics will need extra body to keep the stitches from puckering the material. Medium- and heavyweight woven fabrics do not need any help, but the lighter weight cottons and almost all knit fabrics need to be stiffened. There are many ways to do this: spray-on starch ironed into the fabric sometimes affords enough extra body for intricate stitching. Also, putting a piece of typing paper between the fabric and the needle plate helps. The paper is then gently torn away after stitching (Diagram 14). If you have a large piece of fabric to stitch, adding machine tape can be used. I have seen the use of tissue paper advised for stiffening, but it never works for me, being too soft to keep the fabric from puckering. More often I back fabrics with a piece of organza or lightweight interfacing. You can even draw your design on the organza or interfacing and decorate the piece from the wrong side, as mentioned in Chapter 1.

Before you try a straight stitch on your fabric, run a line of it on your doodle cloth. Remember what a doodle cloth is? Set up a small rectangle of the same fabric you're sewing on and try a line of straight stitch on it. Does it pucker the fabric? Are you happy with the stitch tension? What does it look like if you tighten the top tension? Loosen the top tension? Tighten the bobbin tension? Loosen it? If you have never manipulated your tension settings, this is the time to experiment, because the rest of the book constantly involves adjusting the settings.

Most machines have a midway point for both upper and lower tension settings. When both indicators are set at these midway points, you have what I call a universal tension setting. If you do not know how to loosen your bobbin tension, consult the instruction manual for your sewing machine or ask your dealer.

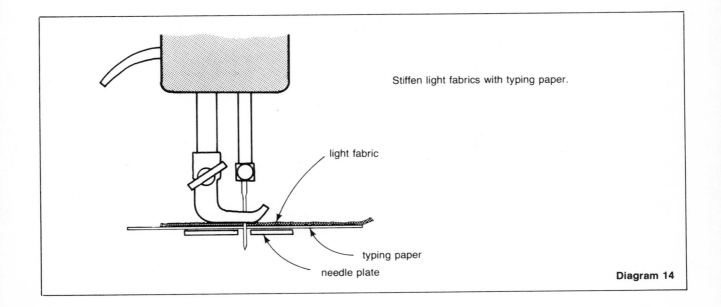

Stiffen light fabrics with typing paper.

light fabric

typing paper

needle plate

Diagram 14

Remember to save yourself a score of headaches by holding the threads together behind the presser foot as you begin to sew. Otherwise, the fabric is sometimes dragged through the needle plate into the bobbin case area, and valuable time and psychic energy is lost in unsnarling the mess. (Diagram 15)

Learning to be comfortable while spending hours at the machine is dependent upon your posture and the

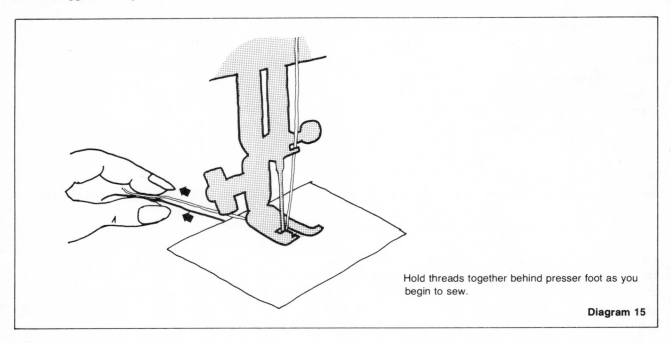

Hold threads together behind presser foot as you begin to sew.

Diagram 15

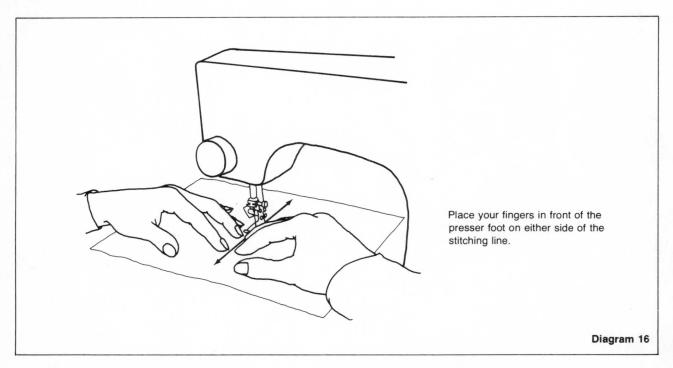

Place your fingers in front of the presser foot on either side of the stitching line.

Diagram 16

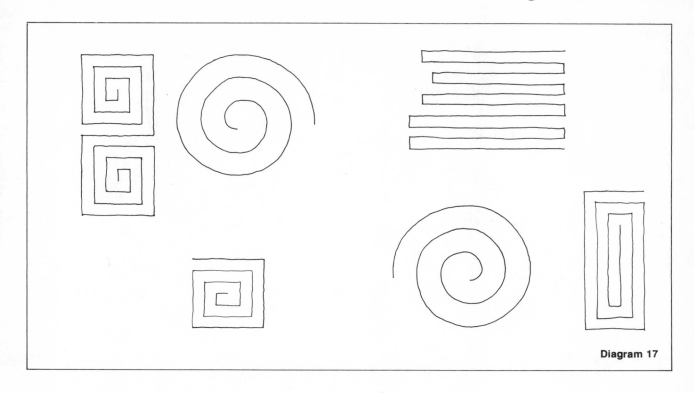

Diagram 17

way you hold your arms and fingers. If you slump, and at the same time work with your elbows flapping in the air like pelican wings, you will have a backache and be exhausted in a short time. Hold yourself erect, with a straight spine, and lean forward from your hips. Rest your elbows on the sewing surface and place your fingers as shown. Don't place your hands and arms parallel to the seam line as it does nasty things to your fabric. (Diagram 16)

The bobbin tension of some machines is preset in the factory. Therefore, the instruction manual will tell you not to fiddle with bobbin tension. If you want to explore the full range of effects possible with machine stitchery, ignore the manufacturer's warning. Specific details on what to do are in Chapter 4. For now, merely manipulate top tension.

If nothing seems to keep the fabric from puckering, put a piece of interfacing or organza under the doodle cloth and try again. As you change the tension settings for the doodle cloth, write them down directly on the cloth (see Plate 3, page 13).

The first time I ever sewed on a machine, I was given a sheet of printed straight lines and spirals, both curved and squared. Using an unthreaded machine, I sewed slowly and carefully along the lines. It taught me to take my time and to watch the stitch that is being formed, at the same time looking ahead to where the needle will enter the fabric next. I learned to vary the speed at which I sewed, slowing for curves, turns, and intricate places, and speeding up on the long lines of straight stitch (Diagram 17). If you have not had much practice with sewing on the machine, you might want to copy the cartoons at the end of each chapter onto typing paper, and then practice stitching the main lines with an unthreaded machine. You could then use the paper to transfer the design to fabric, via the pounce method (see Chapter 1).

For all machine-embroidered garments (except, obviously, ready-made wear), be sure to do the embellishing before you cut out the contours of the pattern piece. To do this, first cut off the excess tissue paper around the pattern piece, anchor it with weights or

a First cut a large rectangle around your garment piece.

b Embellish garment before cutting out the contours.

Diagram 18

pins, or spray-position it to the fabric, and trace around with pencil or tailor's chalk. Remove the pattern piece and cut a large rectangle around the garment, allowing at least two inches of extra fabric all the way around. Transfer your design to the appropriate place on the garment piece and do the stitching. Then press on the wrong side and cut out the actual contours of the garment piece. If any puckering has occurred, you can sometimes make adjustments in cutting out the piece, whereas if you had cut the piece first and then stitched it, the puckering would be unalterable. (Diagram 18)

At last, you may begin stitching! One good use of straight stitch is for appliqué. Cut out your shapes with a ¼"(6mm) seam allowance and then straight stitch along the seam line, so that when you clip the curves and press the seam allowance under, the edge is crisp and neat. Pin the shape to its backing, using lots of pins to keep the fabric from shifting while stitching, and sew ⅛"(3mm) away from the turned edge. Some people prefer to bond their appliqué shapes to the background with fusible web interfacing instead of pinning. (Diagram 19)

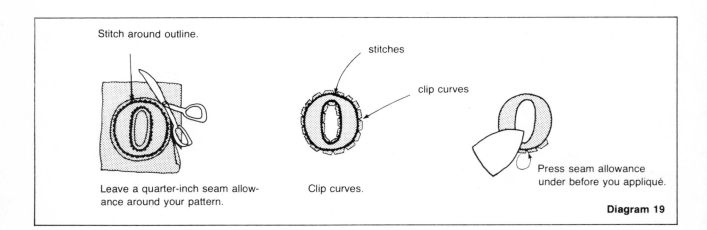

Stitch around outline.

Leave a quarter-inch seam allowance around your pattern.

stitches

clip curves

Clip curves.

Press seam allowance under before you appliqué.

Diagram 19

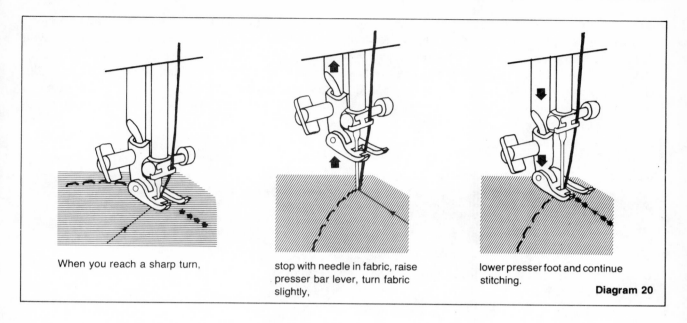

When you reach a sharp turn,

stop with needle in fabric, raise presser bar lever, turn fabric slightly,

lower presser foot and continue stitching.

Diagram 20

By holding your fingers as shown in Diagram 16, you will prevent the fabric from puckering. When you reach sharp turns in the shape, stop the machine with the needle in the fabric, lift the presser bar lever, and turn the fabric slightly so that the presser foot is aimed in the right direction. If you force the fabric under the presser foot at turns, you may stretch the material on the bias, which results in unsightly bulges. (Diagram 20)

Try to cut out your appliqué shapes so that when they are pinned to the backing, the grain lines of both the appliqué and backing are lined up. For example, I once made an appliquéd butterfly, fluttering at an angle on the backing fabric. Instead of cutting out the butterfly on the straight grain of the appliqué fabric, I cut it on the bias so that when I pinned it to the backing, the grains would line up. (Diagram 21)

How do you handle enormous appliqué shapes, say for a bedspread or wall hanging? First of all, work on a flat surface when you are pinning the appliqués to the backing, so everything will lie flat. Pin liberally, so the

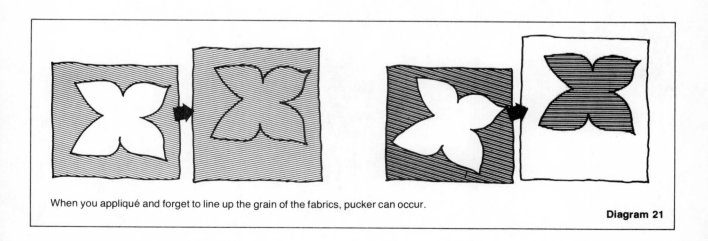

When you appliqué and forget to line up the grain of the fabrics, pucker can occur.

Diagram 21

fabric won't shift as you sew. Keep your hands to the sides of the fabric, using your fingers as guides, as shown above. You can backstitch the first and last stitches, but I prefer to pull the ends to the back and tie off in knots. When you have a large number of ends to finish, however, you may want to pull them to the back and put a spot of fabric glue on them, which will hold through continual washings.

Crosshatching is an easy way to fill in large areas with color or texture, and is done by laying intersecting lines of straight stitching on top of each other in a grid. The description of how to crosshatch is accurate, but dense. Study the pictures and try not to be boggled by the text, which makes a very easy maneuver sound complex.

Stitch down a line. At the bottom, leave the needle in

Plate 5
To crosshatch, stitch a line of straight stitch. Leave the needle in the fabric and pivot the material another 90° counterclockwise.

Lower the presser bar lever and stitch one or two stitches, leaving the needle in the fabric and pivoting the material another 90°. Continue crosshatching in this manner.

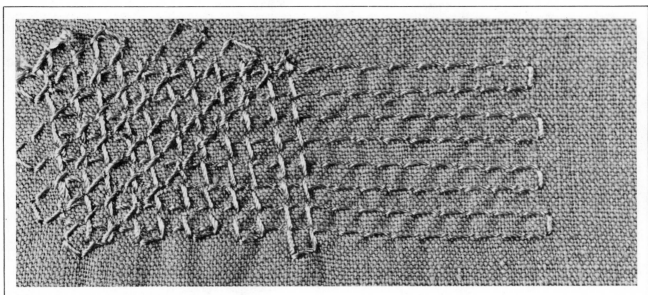

Plate 6 Rectangle in three stages of crosshatching.

the fabric, raise the presser bar lever, turn the fabric 90°, and lower the presser bar lever. Take one or two stitches. Repeat the procedure by leaving the needle in the fabric, raising the presser bar lever, turning another 90°, lowering the presser bar lever, and stitching another long line of stitches. Use your presser foot as a spacing guide between rows of stitches. It's hard to declare how far the second line should be away from the first line because the length of your stitches at the bottom of each row determines how far away you will be from the first row of stitching. Maintain this spacing to keep your lines parallel. When you have finished a rectangle of parallel stitches, turn the fabric 90° and stitch rows of straight stitch, perpendicular to the previous rows. (Plates 5 and 6)

It is annoying to run out of bobbin thread halfway through crosshatching a project, so start with a full bobbin.

Crosshatching can also be done in an irregular manner by using the backstitch lever on a machine. (Plate 7)

Since we use a straight-stitch crosshatching for texture, choose a thread that has some sheen to catch the light. If you do row upon row of stitching with 100%

cotton, the effect will be lost and you might as well use checked fabric. But if you use polyester, thin silk, or rayon thread and perhaps play with color changes, you create the vibrant feeling characteristic of all embroidery.

Without thinking clearly, I tried filling in small shapes, such as initials and little flowerpots, with crosshatching, and nearly pulled out all my hair with many irregular turns and twists. Then I realized that it would be easier to make a large rectangle of crosshatching, with long lines of stitching, than to fill in small shapes. After bonding a piece of iron-on interfacing to the back of this rectangle, I now cut out my shapes and appliqué them by machine to a backing. The iron-on interfacing keeps the edges from fraying. Because this works particularly well for lettering, the project at the end of the chapter uses this method. If you design the letters to touch each other, you can appliqué them in one operation, as if they were script. (Diagram 22)

Some people like to use cello-tape instead of pins to hold appliqué to a backing, stitching right through the tape and later pulling it off. I cannot recommend cello-taping these letters to the backing when the edge is so vulnerable to fraying. When you pull the

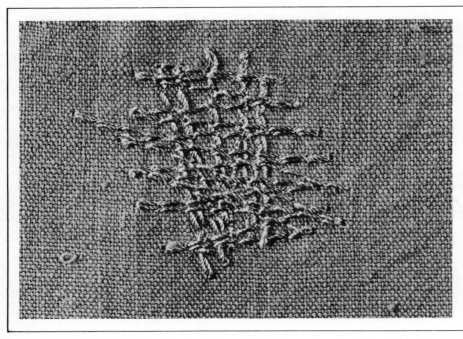

Plate 7
Crosshatching done in an irregular manner with the backstitch lever.

o's . . .

- learn how a stitch is formed
- understand what can go wrong and why
- prepare your fabric by pre-shrinking it
- hold the threads as you begin to sew
- learn to use your fingers as tools
- embellish before cutting out a garment

AND DON'TS

- hold your hands parallel to the seam line
- force the fabric under the foot at turns
- start a major project of crosshatching with a half-full bobbin
- use cello-tape on frayable fabrics

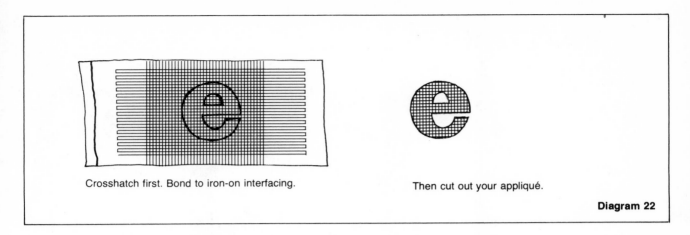

Crosshatch first. Bond to iron-on interfacing.

Then cut out your appliqué.

Diagram 22

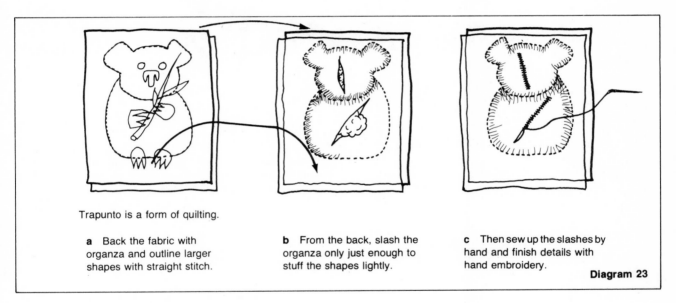

Trapunto is a form of quilting.

a Back the fabric with organza and outline larger shapes with straight stitch.

b From the back, slash the organza only just enough to stuff the shapes lightly.

c Then sew up the slashes by hand and finish details with hand embroidery.

Diagram 23

tape off, it destroys your bonded edge. But cello-tape works well for nonwovens like leather and vinyl.

Quilting with the presser foot on is best done for items with straight lines or broad, sweeping curves. Otherwise, the fabric begins to creep and before long, puckers will be caught on the front and back of the piece. (If your machine has adjustable presser foot tension, use it; also see Chapter 12 for quilting with the darning foot). I recently quilted an enormous piece of striped fabric for a king-sized bedspread. I worked on a pingpong table to support the fabric and loosened both top and bottom tensions slightly to accommodate the extra thickness of top, batting, and bottom. I also stitched on top of adding machine tape to keep the fabric from creeping.

Another form of quilting in selected areas is called trapunto. Back a fabric with organza and straight stitch around a shape on the topside of the fabric. Turn the fabric over and slit the organza only. Stuff batting, felt, or yarn (depending on whether the article is washable or not) into the opening and pad the area evenly. Sew up the slash in the organza by hand, using a whipstitch or a catchstitch. (Diagram 23)

THE PROJECT

Sewing Machine Cover

(pictured in Color Plate 4)

Since dust is the enemy of all machines, an appropriate first project for the straight stitcher is a sewing machine cover. This will give you practice in crosshatching and appliqué.

---

you will need

½ yd. (0,50m) red fabric (I used linen), 35″ (90cm) (or wider), to be backed with:

½ yd. (0,50m) nonwoven interfacing

1¼ yds. (1,15m) ready-made corded red piping

1¼ yds. (1,15m) double-fold red bias tape

white light-weight cotton, 8½″ (21,8cm) square

iron-on interfacing, 9″ (23cm) square

one spool each, blue, white, and red, cotton-covered polyester thread

scissors, tissue paper, felt-tip pen, pins or spray-on pattern holder

doodle cloth of white fabric

step-by-step:

1 Trace the letters onto the tissue paper. (Diagram 24)

2 Load the machine with blue thread, top and bottom.

3 On the doodle cloth of the white fabric, try a line of straight stitch with a stitch length of 10-12 stitches per inch. If the tension is right and the material does not pucker, you are ready to sew on the white fabric. Otherwise, adjust the tensions until you're happy with the results. Mark all changes directly on the doodle cloth for future reference.

4 On the white fabric, draw a rectangle, 8½″ (21,8cm) by 8½″ square, with a pencil.

5 Crosshatch the rectangle with blue thread. Sew down the right side of the rectangle until you reach the bottom. Leaving the needle in the fabric, raise the presser bar lever, turn the fabric 90°, lower the presser bar lever, and hand turn the wheel one stitch. Leaving the needle in the fabric, raise the presser bar lever, turn the fabric 90°, lower the presser bar lever, and sew another long line.

6 Continue until you have filled in all the vertical lines of the rectangle. Then begin filling in the horizontal lines.

7 Press the rectangle from the back. Then carefully lay a slightly smaller rectangle of iron-on interfacing

Diagram 24

over the back of the crosshatched fabric. Press until the two fabrics are securely bonded. Wait a few minutes for the fabric to cool off so the bond will be strong.

8 Pin the letters, one by one, to the crosshatching and cut them out carefully. Be sure to leave as little waste space as possible between letters; otherwise you will not have enough for all the letters. Also be sure the crosshatching lines are parallel to the sides of the letters.

9 Cut a rectangle of red linen, 22″ (56cm) x 16½″ (41,8cm). Back it with a rectangle of interfacing, machine basting the two together ¼″ (6mm) from the edges. NOTE: If you have a free-arm machine, this rectangle will be too short. Measure your machine and before cutting the linen, add the appropriate inches to the bottoms of the three pattern pieces (main body plus two sides).

10 Trace the side pattern onto tissue paper and cut two from both the linen and the interfacing. Back each side piece with interfacing, machine-basting ¼″ (6mm) from the edge. (Diagram 24)

11 Pin the letters to main body. "Machine" should stretch all the way from one seam line to the other, with the bottom of the letters 2″ (5cm) from the bottom of the sewing machine cover. The letters should touch. The bottom of the letters for "sewing" should be 5½″ (14cm) from the bottom of the sewing machine cover, with the "g" above the "e" in "machine."

12 Load the machine with white thread, top and bottom, and sew the letters to the red linen. Since the letters of each word are touching, you can sew them in one operation, as if they were written in script.

13 Load the machine with red thread, top and bottom, and put the cording or zipper foot on the machine. Sew the piping to the side pattern pieces, then clip the curved corners. Pin the main body of the cover to the side inserts, right sides together, matching centers. (Don't tell anybody, but I hand-basted them together for a perfect fit.) Clip the edge of the main body where the curved corners will fall and stitch the pieces together. Turn to the right side and press the seams.

14 Sew double-folded bias tape to the bottom edge.

ADDITIONAL IDEAS

■ Change the letters of this chapter's design and make a cover for a typewriter, blender, adding machine, or coffee-maker.

■ Make a fabric sign to be hung on a child's door ("Kali's room," or "Keep out").

■ Appliqué large colorful shapes to canvas to make a child's fabric play tent (two lengths of PVC sprinkler pipe can be used as inside supports).

SUMMARY OF TECHNIQUES

| | stitch | | tensions | | | | |
	width	length	top	bobbin	foot	feed dog	comments
straight stitch	0	any	universal		presser	in place	
crosshatching	0	10–12	universal		presser	in place	see Diag. 19
quilting	0	10–12	loosen	loosen	presser	in place	stitch on top of adding machine tape
trapunto	0	10–12	universal		presser	in place	see Diag. 23

■ Sew a person's name in script (see Diagram 29) on fabric backed with oganza. Pad lightly (see directions for trapunto), line, and use as a pocket on ready-made clothing.

■ Crosshatch in icy blue and cut out the word "January," appliquéing it to a canvas rectangle that is the beginning of a fabric calendar, and that will also serve as a sampler of the techniques you're learning. Watch the Additional Ideas section at the end of each chapter for the coming months.

THREE

SIMPLE ZIGZAG

GLOSSARY

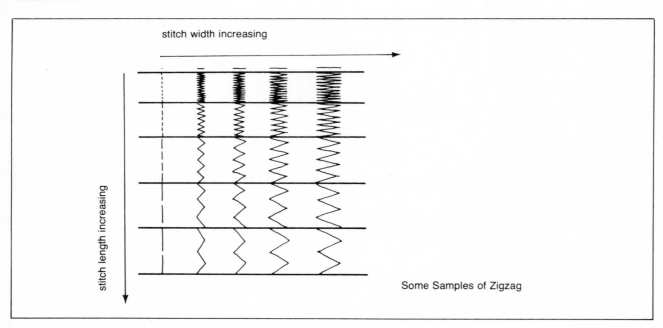

stitch width increasing

stitch length increasing

Some Samples of Zigzag

THE TECHNIQUE

Those of us fortunate enough to have a zigzag sewing machine know the joys and potential of this comparatively new invention—sewing lingerie and bathing suits, overcasting seams, making knit outfits. But the possibilities of simple zigzag in decorative machine embroidery have been relatively unexplored.

And yet by playing with the bobbin and upper tensions, and by changing both the stitch length and width, we can achieve a variety of intriguing yet easy-to-do effects.

For example, look at the differences between ordinary zigzag on medium-weight cotton at normal tension settings, and zigzag with the upper tension tightened to its highest setting. Below these samples are differences in length of stitch and in loosening of the bobbin tension. Doesn't this variation resemble Feather Stitch in hand embroidery and wouldn't it make a lovely border? (Plate 8)

Another effect possible with simple zigzag is called beading, which means to bring the bottom thread to the surface by tightening upper tension and to work the zigzag closely together in a satin stitch. If a contrasting color of thread is wound into the bobbin, interesting color play can highlight your work. In the caftans below, the turquoise thread is beaded at the sides of the zigzag in brown. Some machines have a special way to achieve beading, but for most machines, you will have to experiment on a doodle cloth to find the upper and lower tension settings that bring the bobbin thread precisely to the surface and not beyond. Remember that every time you stop your machine, the bobbin thread is brought *farther* to the surface than it would in the process of stitching, so that when you start up again, there is the bobbin thread in the middle of your zigzag instead of behaving itself on the side. Remedy this by planning beading in a straight or widely curving line in order to sew an entire line without stopping the machine.

We made a crosshatched sewing machine cover in Chapter 2 and this same technique can be done in

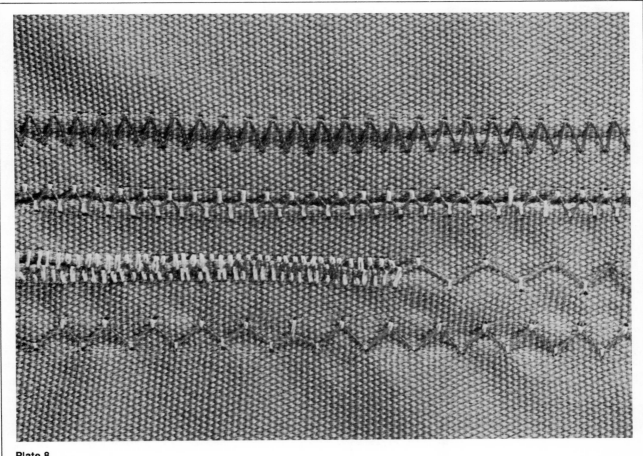

Plate 8

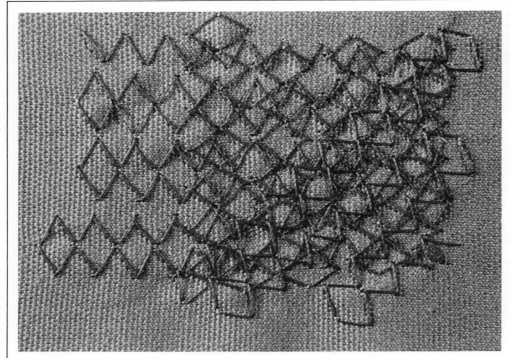

zigzag. Be careful that your tension is not too tight or the fabric will pucker. If you need to cover large areas fast, zigzag crosshatching does the job. (Plate 9)

When you find the position on your stitch length dial or lever that gives you an acceptable satin stitch (which is a tightly packed zigzag), mark the position with your pen so that you can find this hallowed place again——even 1/16th of an inch (1,5mm) variation in setting makes a difference.

The trick is to find the place that pulls your fabric through the presser foot without either destroying the solid line of zigzag stitching, or letting threads pile up so much that the presser foot cannot climb over the mess. Again, practice on your doodle cloth. Sew rapidly . . . but not recklessly because your thread will break (and you gave up swearing for Lent). A plastic see-through embroidery foot has grooves under it for climbing easily over rows of satin stitch and is useful for heavily decorated items.

Speaking of acceptable satin stitches, there is a secret to the perfect machine satin stitch. For years I

have been frustrated with the coarseness and sloppiness of my satin stitches, but I finally learned the trick: use extra-fine thread. If your favorite fabric store does not carry it, see the Supply List at the end of the book.

As for width of satin stitch, I usually select the third widest setting on my machine, a personal quirk. Somehow a satin stitch in that widest setting never looks neat enough for me.

Turning satin stitch corners takes some practice before you reach perfection. As you come to the end of a zigzag line, imagine that you are building a swimming pool wall. Keep your needle on the outside edge of your wall as you turn—e.g., if the wall turns left, your needle will stop in the fabric at the right-hand corner. Lift the presser foot, turn the fabric counterclockwise 90°, put down the presser foot, and merrily stitch, watching carefully that the foot is not catching on the extra layer of thread at the corner. (Plate 10)

Zigzag can be hard on lightweight cotton, puckering it badly. In most cases where the fabric needs extra body, you can pin a piece of typing paper on the back of

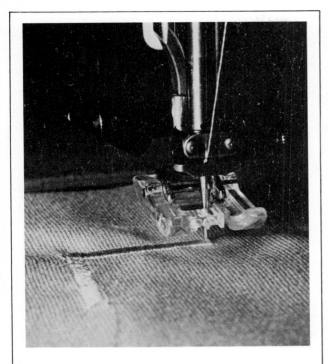

Plate 10 To turn a satin stitch corner, keep the needle on the outside edge as you pivot the material. You can see the two grooves on the underside of the embroidery foot which help it to pass smoothly over previous rows of satin stitch.

machines have a dial or special lever arrangement to allow slipping back and forth from the 0 setting to the 4. Changing these settings at regular intervals produces a variety of line (Plate 11). To insure regularity without spending an hour measuring and marking intervals, machine-baste a straight line (longest stitch length setting) and cover up every other basting stitch with wide vari-width zigzag.

How to handle goofs? Practicing on the doodle cloth prevents 90% of them, but if you make a mistake, rip stitches from the underside to a corner or intersection. Remove excess threads on the topside. Begin anew with your needle on the outside corner of the turn, holding the two threads securely in your hands, and with the stitch width lever set to 0. Take a few stitches to lock the threads but don't allow the material to move. Reset the stitch width lever to whatever your setting was and continue stitching as before. The new stitches will lock the ends of the old ones.

Save your doodle cloth; you never know when you will need it again and it can save you hours of experimenting. Label it with the pattern and size number and pin it to the pattern.

the fabric and stitch through both layers. You can also loosen both upper and lower tensions. Some sources advise the use of tissue paper. Here are two objections: it doesn't work and it's hard to extract the paper. I once made a rainbow of zigzag and decorative stitches on see-through silk organza. *Smart me,* I thought, *I'll back this with old pattern tissue for extra body.* When I finished, not only did the printed sewing directions on the pattern paper show through the organza, but I spent hours picking out shreds of tissue paper. One way to circumvent those hours is to wet the piece, dissolving the tissue.

The last effect we will explore with simple zigzag before launching you into a project is called vari-width zigzag, which means to change the stitch width lever from the narrowest setting (0, or a straight line) to the widest and back again after a few stitches. Some

Plate 11 Vari-width zigzag can be staggered to give interesting effects

⎲o's . . .

- complete your zigzag decoration before cutting out the pattern
- practice on a doodle cloth, labelling your experiments as you go
- sew smoothly and rapidly . . . but not recklessly
- mark the best stitch length position on *your* machine for satin stitch
- back lightweight fabrics with interfacing to prevent puckering
- hold on to the top and bobbin threads when you begin sewing

AND DON'TS

- start and stop your machine stitching when beading
- plan beading for designs that turn corners

HIS & HERS CAFTANS

(pictured in Color Plate 6)

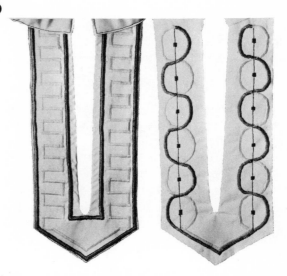

Now you are ready to exercise your new knowledge about zigzag. The His & Hers Caftans were designed to include practice in beading, satin stitch with lots of corners, and vari-width zigzag.

you will need:

patterns for men's and women's caftans

8 yds. (7,35m) of brown fabric

½ yd. (0,50m) of cream fabric

1 spool each of gold, turquoise, and brown extra-fine 100% cotton thread

lightweight nonwoven interfacing

tracing paper

pencil, ruler, tailor's chalk, felt-tip pen, tape, pins or spray-on pattern holder

a doodle cloth

step-by-step for His Caftan:

1 Cut off excess tissue paper around the front tab pattern piece and pin it on (or spray-position it to) the cream fabric. Trace around the edges of the pattern with a pencil and mark the center slit lines. Remove the tab pattern piece.

2 On the pattern measure the width of one side of the tab from side *seam* line to center *seam* line. Find the halfway point (on my pattern, ¼" [2cm]) from the outside seam line) and mark it on the cream fabric with a light dotted line of tailor's chalk, the entire length of each side of the front tab. Draw another line across the bottom of the fabric where the two outside edges begin to angle towards each other. These lines are merely register lines to help you in accurately transferring the design from the book to your fabric. If the center slit line of the tab on your pattern tapers, thereby increasing

the measurement of the tab's width from top to bottom, take a measurement at the bottom of the tab to insure that the design will fit your space.

3 Cut a large rectangle of cream fabric surrounding the tab—not so big you'll have trouble handling it on the machine, and not so small you can't grasp it comfortably while working.

4 Place tracing paper (outdated pattern tissue paper is perfect) over the cartoon (Diagram 25) and copy the design with a heavy line—black felt-tip pen, for example. Be sure to let the ink dry before the next step, so you won't smudge the back of your fabric.

5 Tape the tracing paper to a window and position and tape your cream fabric over it, matching the centering and bottom lines. Because hand-drawn straight lines often look sloppy, use a ruler (or the edge of a book) and a pencil to draw perfectly straight lines. For the Roman border on the insides of the straight lines, also use the ruler, but skip at appropriate intervals. (Note: You don't have to copy the design this way, but it's handy and fast.)

6 Baste a rectangle of lightweight interfacing to the back of the cream fabric to give your work body and to prevent it from puckering.

7 Cut a doodle cloth, also backed by interfacing, and be sure the grain of the fabric on your doodle cloth runs the same as on the garment tab—in this case, the stitching runs perpendicular to, or crosses, the lengthwise grain.

8 Load your machine, both top and bobbin, with extra-fine gold thread. Be sure your needle is the right size in relation to your fabric. Set the stitch length at the mark you made earlier for the perfect satin stitch. Set stitch width at next to widest, or whatever is most attractive to you.

9 Experiment with tension settings on your doodle cloth and remember to mark the settings directly on the doodle cloth fabric. If your fabric tends to pucker, loosen both the top and bottom tensions. After fiddling around, I found that my best setting for satin stitch on *this* fabric is universal tension.

10 Starting on the left tab and holding the two threads securely as you start, stitch the inside Roman border, remembering that when the fabric pivots, your needle should be on the outside edge (left, when you turn right; and right, when you turn left).

11 Change the bobbin to brown thread and the upper to turquoise. Practice on your doodle cloth until you have a good beading effect. I tightened my upper tension to 7 and loosened the lower to 0.

12 Stitch the inside line of beading, remembering to sew smoothly with as few stops as possible. Next sew the outside line of beading.

13 Press, trim off excess fabric, and finish garment construction, topstitching collar and tab if desired.

step-by-step for Her Caftan:

1 Follow the same steps as in His Caftan, through step 6, copying the design for Hers, of course (Diagram 26). You do not need a new doodle cloth, if you have already marked the old one.

2 Load both the top and bobbin of your machine with turquoise thread and set the width and length for satin stitch. Now draw about 3″ (7,5cm) of the design on the doodle cloth and practice executing those wide turns smoothly before tackling the actual garment.

3 When you have mastered this technique, sew the turquoise line, beginning on the left side and holding the two threads securely as you start.

4 Load gold thread in both the top and bobbin to stitch the other side of the curving lines. Beware of a buildup of threads where the two lines cross.

5 Load brown thread in both top and bobbin. On your doodle cloth, practice flipping the stitch width lever from 0 to the widest setting and back to 0.

6 When you have mastered the vari-width zigzag, stitch down the center line you marked in tailor's chalk on the tab, increasing to a wide stitch in the middle of the bulges and decreasing to 0 when you cross the intersections. If you want absolute regularity, make a cardboard or paper template of one of the bulges, find the center, and cut a small rectangle out of the center. Place the template on each bulge and mark on the center line the upper and lower boundaries of the widest stitch in your line of vari-width zigzag.

7 Press, trim off excess fabric, and finish garment construction, topstitching collar and tab if desired.

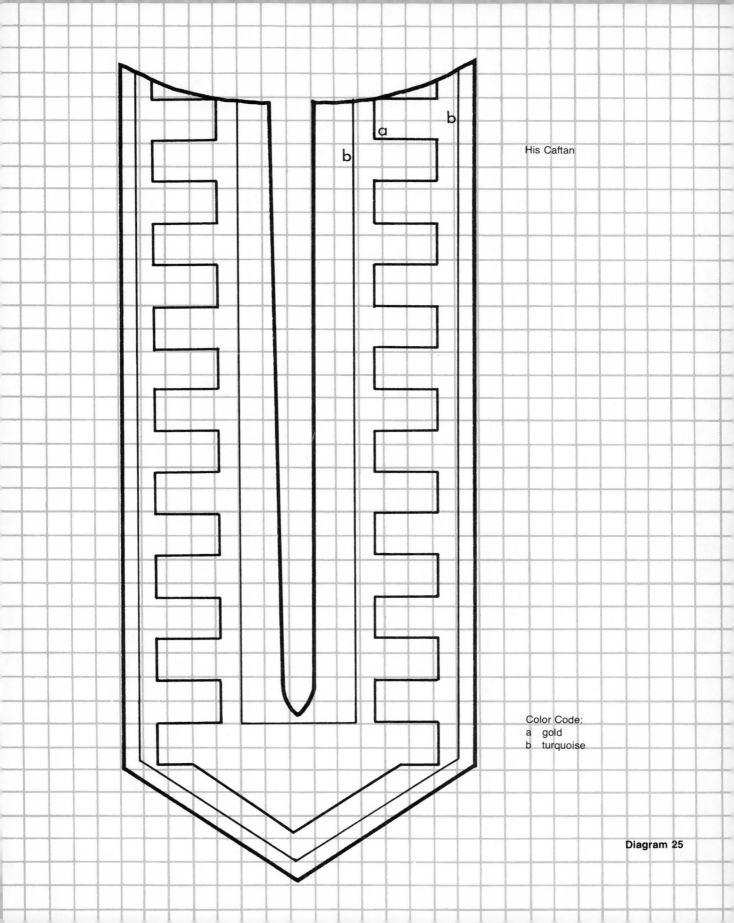

His Caftan

Color Code:
a gold
b turquoise

Diagram 25

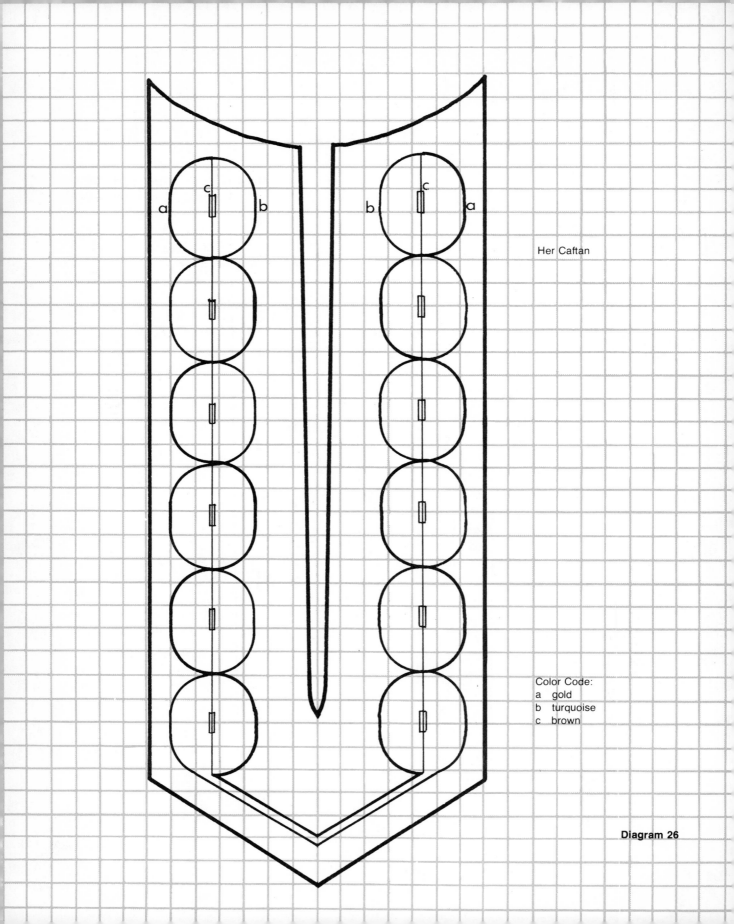

Her Caftan

Color Code:
a   gold
b   turquoise
c   brown

Diagram 26

ADDITIONAL IDEAS

■ Use the chapter's designs as a pillow case border.

■ Combine open zigzag with rows of rickrack on a ready-made skirt.

■ Make a rajah's stuffed elephant with sumptuous satin stitched blankets and heavily machine-embroidered ears (do the work first before cutting out the animal).

■ Proclaim a family gathering with a banner on which everyone's name is stitched in satin stitch letters.

■ Make a pink satin stitched "February" beaded with red bobbin thread. Crosshatch a rectangle with red rayon thread, bond iron-on interfacing to the back, cut out hearts, and appliqué them around February on your fabric calendar. (See Chapter 2—Additional Ideas, if you don't understand.)

SUMMARY OF TECHNIQUES

	stitch		tensions			
	width	length	top	bobbin	foot	feed dog
open zigzag (zz)	1–4	10–12	universal		presser	in place
satin stitch	1–4	fine	loosen	regular	embroidery	in place
beading	1–4	fine	tighten	loosen	embroidery	in place
crosshatching (zz)	1–4	10–12	universal		presser	in place
vari-width (zz)	1–4	fine	universal		embroidery	in place

FOUR
FREE MACHINE EMBROIDERY WITH HOOP

GLOSSARY

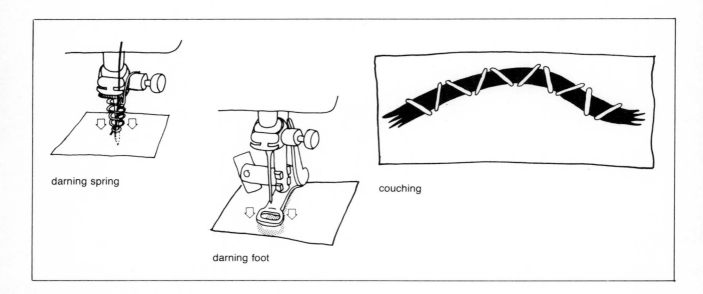

darning spring

darning foot

couching

THE TECHNIQUE

Fun and exciting are the two words I've heard most often about free machine embroidery, a term which means to remove the presser foot, to lower or cover the feed dogs, and to move the fabric freely in any direction while stitching.

People who are not comfortable drawing with a pencil usually blossom with free machine embroidery, achieving spontaneous effects they'd never dreamed they could.

Preparation of each machine is slightly different and the best way to find out what's right for your machine is to read your machine's instruction book and to talk to your sewing machine dealer. Follow the same instructions as for darning. You need to know whether you can lower the feed dogs on your machine, where the bobbin tension screw is and how to tighten or loosen it, and how to bypass the bobbin tension altogether.

Below is a brief chart of the major brands and how to adapt them to free machine embroidery.

If your brand is not listed here, look in the yellow pages of your telephone directory for the address of your nearest dealer.

Remember that there is more than one way to adapt your machine to free machine embroidery and the only way to find out what works best for you is to experiment. When I started with free machine embroidery, everyone told me that you *had* to lower the feed dogs. For a while I was paralyzed because there's no way to do that on my machine.

Then I realized that darning is similar to free machine embroidery, so I put the darning plate over my feed dogs, and the darning foot on instead of the presser foot. Naturally I didn't follow my own advice

about practicing on a doodle cloth and plunged in to work on a huge banner for my mother. To my utter frustration, about every two minutes the darning plate popped off and if I didn't notice it immediately, the needle soon struck loose metal and broke. Later, my favorite sewing machine dealer calmly pointed out that the stitch length dial *must* be set at 0 or the feed dogs move back and forth, dislodging the darning plate. (I never finished the banner either.) (Diagram 27)

Meanwhile, before I discovered this secret, I was so spitting mad at the darning plate that I took it off permanently . . . and found out that it didn't make any difference whether the feed dogs were lowered, covered, or otherwise hidden. As long as I put on the darning foot—which holds the fabric down during the formation of each stitch and thereby prevents skipped stitches, broken thread, and snapped needles—I could freely stitch. Others with different brands of machines have told me the same. They don't bother to lower the feed dogs at all; the removal of the presser foot and some way to hold the fabric taut immediately

	Feed Dogs	Bypassing Bobbin Tension
Bernina	drop	thread through hole in bobbin case
Brother	drop	loosen only; cannot bypass
Elna	cover	thread through hole in back of case
JC Penney	drop	thread through hole in bobbin case
Kenmore (Sears')	drop	thread through hole in bobbin case
Morse	varies	varies*
Necchi	drop	loosen only; cannot bypass
Nelco	varies	varies
New Home	varies	varies
Pfaff	drop	loosen only; cannot bypass
Riccar	drop	thread through tiny wire spring
Singer	raise plate to darning position	loosen only; cannot bypass
Viking	drop	thread through hole in bobbin case
White	drop	thread through wire spring

*Models vary; sometimes a class 15 bobbin case with a bypass hole can be purchased for machines that ordinarily do not have a bypass hole.

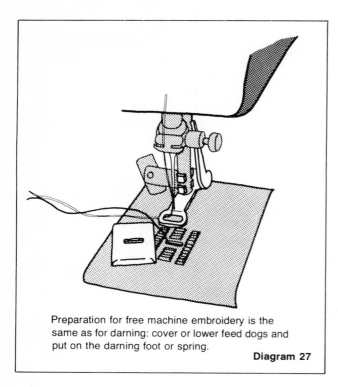

Preparation for free machine embroidery is the same as for darning: cover or lower feed dogs and put on the darning foot or spring.

Diagram 27

last goes the bottom of the hoop (Diagram 28). Push the inner ring ⅛″ (3mm) below the outer ring for a snug fit. It also helps to wrap the rings of the embroidery hoop with strips of cotton fabric, bias binding, or electrical tape to keep the fabric from slipping. There are special machine embroidery hoops that have an indentation on the wood and are not very deep, both to allow easy slipping of the hoop under the needle. However these hoops are hard to find (check the Supply List at the end of the book). You can file a half-moon on the upper and lower edge of your embroidery hoop if it's too thick to go under the needle. You can also tip the hoop on its side and slide it carefully under the needle—or merely take off the needle while sliding the hoop under the presser bar lever, and then put it back on.

You *can* free machine embroider with no foot on the machine (with the fabric in a hoop), but if ever you were destined to sew together your fingers, this would be the time. To be on the safe, unpainful side, I recommend always using the darning foot for free machine embroidery. (Some machines use a darning spring rather than a foot.)

Check your set-up against mine: I have medium-weight cotton fabric in a 6″(15cm)-diameter embroidery hoop; a Size 12 (80) needle, and ordinary 100% cotton sewing machine thread (two different colors in

around the needle (hoop, fingers, darning foot, etc.) works perfectly well. So experiment on your machine and have fun while you do.

It is extremely important to match the correct size needle with, and to choose an appropriate thread for, the fabric you are practicing on, so consult the Needle and Thread Chart on page 190. Briefly, you can do free machine embroidery on almost any fabric, although tightly woven fabrics are sometimes more difficult to work on, and without care, knits tend to stretch. You can always back these fabrics with typing paper or lightweight interfacing before putting them in the hoop (tear off the paper after stitching).

Practice free machine embroidery on some medium-weight cotton with two different upper and lower colored threads, so that you can easily judge whether your bobbin thread is loose or tight. You will use an ordinary 6″ (15cm) or 8″ (20,5cm) wood or plastic embroidery hoop, but you will put it on backwards—that is, the top part of the hoop with the screw goes on the bottom; next comes the fabric; and

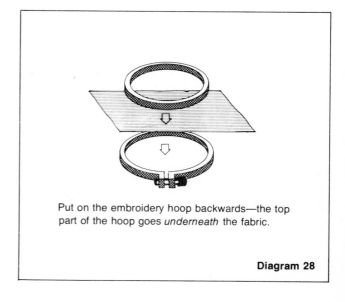

Put on the embroidery hoop backwards—the top part of the hoop goes *underneath* the fabric.

Diagram 28

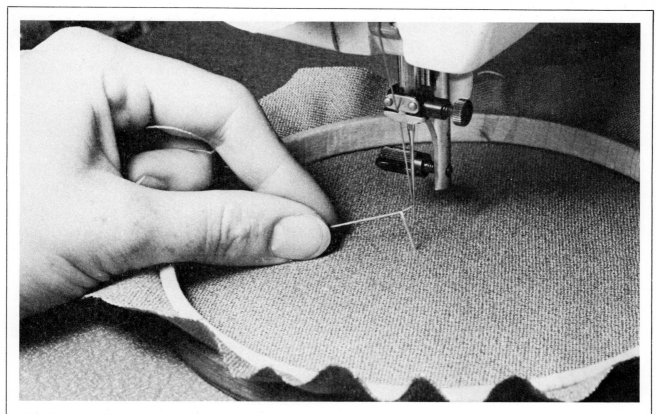

Plate 12 To lock the initial stitch, hold the upper thread in your left hand and draw up the bobbin thread. Take three or four stitches in the same place and cut off ends.

top and bottom); stitch length set at 0; darning foot on. Because I will be moving the hoop vigorously, I've put the extensions on my free-arm to make a large flat working surface.

All right, your machine is ready, your fabric stretched in the hoop, and you're ready to experiment. Setting the needle at its highest point, slide the hoop under the needle. My hoop is only ⅜"(1cm) thick; if yours is deeper, you may need to take off the darning foot first, slide the hoop under the needle, and then put on the darning foot. And don't forget to lower the presser foot lever. This lever controls upper tension—and I could kick myself every time I have forgotten to depress the lever, only to rip out unwanted loops in the upper thread.

First, *always,* you need to lock the initial stitch. Hold the thread in your left hand, hand-turn the wheel to make one stitch, and draw up the bobbin thread. Holding the two threads firmly, take about three stitches in the same hole. You have now locked that first stitch and can cut off the two threads. Be careful not to cut the wrong threads, which I've (grumble, snarl) done a million times. Sometimes I wait to cut the threads until I've stitched several inches away from them.(Plate 12)

Now try writing your name in thread. Place your hands firmly around the hoop, keeping your index and middle fingers near the needle (but without impaling them). Do this, because at the moment the needle enters the fabric, the material *must* be pressed against the needle plate or a stitch cannot be formed. I keep my pinkies and thumbs outside the hoop and move the whole affair with all my fingers pressing firmly but not

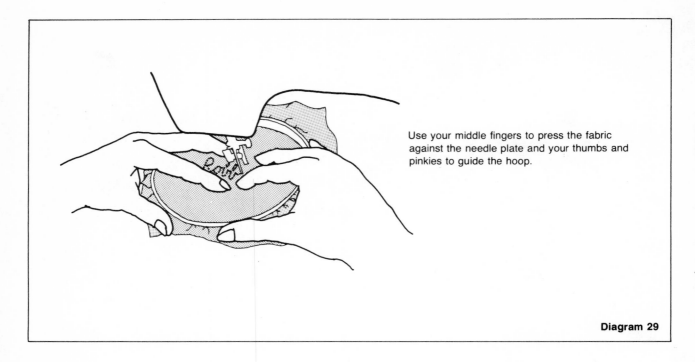

Use your middle fingers to press the fabric against the needle plate and your thumbs and pinkies to guide the hoop.

Diagram 29

tensely against the cloth. Remember, *you* move the fabric, since there are no presser feet or feed dogs to guide it. Exciting, isn't it! (Diagram 29)

Oh, your needle just broke? That's because you're moving the fabric too fast, taking giant, jerky stitches and thereby bending the needle so that it does not enter the hole in the needle plate, striking metal instead. Slow down a little and try not to jerk the hoop around. So what if you take two stitches in the same place. Of course, if you take too many stitches in the same place, the thread will also break.

Try every movement you can dream up—forwards, backwards, sidewards, loops, spirals, squares, ogees (what?). At some point you will be backing up—and bang, run into the side of the hoop—what to do? Turn the hoop, of course; you can write your name upside-down or backwards in free machine embroidery.

Now let's try some special effects. By manipulating bobbin and thread tensions, and by changing the weight of cloth stitched on, a whole range of beautiful effects can be achieved. For example, by loosening the bobbin tension and not messing with upper at all, we can work a line similar to couching in hand em-

broidery. I like to use this effect with gold sewing machine thread. The left half of the photo is worked on medium-weight cotton, the right on wool. (Plate 13)

It is also possible to bypass the tension spring completely, allowing you to use quite heavy thread in the bobbin (6-stranded embroidery floss, linen carpet warp, handspun wool, etc.—how to handle these is covered in Chapter 6), and to bring the bobbin thread up to the surface in large loops, called a whip stitch. Whip stitch is an easy way to give subtle texture to your work and it's twice as pretty if you use two different colors on top and bottom. Because it puckers the lighter fabrics badly, always use a hoop for this stitch. (Plate 14)

Bypassing bobbin tension is different on each machine; again, check the chart on page 49. Bobbin cases have either one or two screws. When there are two, the one on the left usually holds the whole thing together, and the one on the right is the tension screw. Turn it clockwise to tighten bobbin tension and counterclockwise to loosen. If you must loosen a screw to release the bobbin tension, place a piece of felt or other material under the bobbin case on the table to

Plate 13

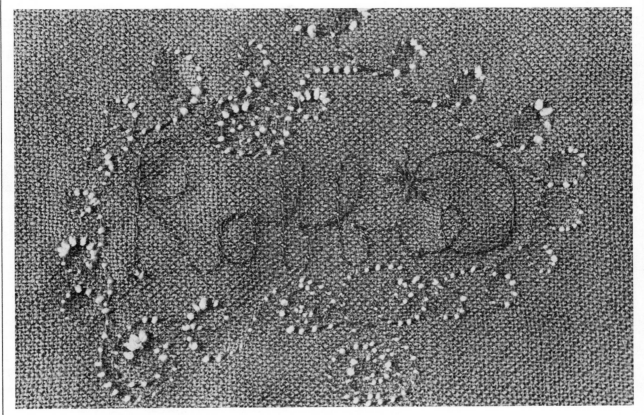

Plate 14   Crochet cotton has been wound onto the bobbin and bobbin tension
bypassed to bring the heavy thread to the surface in loops.

prevent the screw from falling out, bouncing off the table, and secreting itself in your shag rug. My machine has a hole in the (stationary) bobbin case through which I pass the end of the thread if I want to bypass bobbin tension.

Those of you with factory preset bobbin tension should consider buying a second bobbin case, to be marked with nail polish and used only for machine embroidery. The cases for some machines are expensive but will enable you to greatly extend your range of possible effects.

To whip stitch, tighten your upper tension (9 or the tightest position works best for me), and loosen or bypass bobbin tension. Your fabric is still in a hoop, the stitch length at 0, and the darning foot on. Working whip stitch in spirals and loops pulls the bobbin thread into a pleasing flower-like form (and the back is nice too). It may be silly, but I've found making the spirals and loops counterclockwise works better for me. When you are first practicing, if your bobbin thread only breaks once, you receive an A+. (When it doesn't break at all, you graduate with honors.) Why does the thread break? See Chapter 2 for a detailed discussion, but briefly you are probably moving the frame too fast. You will have more loops on each petal if you move the frame slowly, and more spikes if you move it fast. (Diagram 30)

Begin whip stitch in the center of the flower and spiral out to a petal. Stitch each petal in counterclockwise loops.

Diagram 30

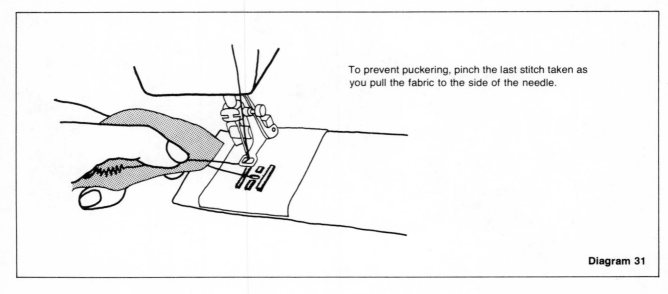

To prevent puckering, pinch the last stitch taken as you pull the fabric to the side of the needle.

Diagram 31

In designing your own work, either clump your flowers very close together or plan to tie off the threads at the end of each flower, as a trail of whip stitch on the surface of your fabric from one flower to the next can look busy and messy. Also, whip stitch does not cover printed fabric solidly, so design accordingly. In the project at the end of this chapter, the flowers were worked on white fabric first and then appliquéd to the gingham. Also, I found the ferns worked with cotton thread did not stand out enough, so I reworked them with heavy (size D) pure silk twist (which means the pillow must be drycleaned because silk twist is not guaranteed colorfast).

Be careful as you draw your fabric away from the needle to cut off threads for tying; if you do not pinch the last stitch taken and pull the fabric gently to the side of the needle, the threads may draw up and pucker the fabric. (Diagram 31)

Last, reset your tension settings to universal and your stitch length to its normal setting.

*D*o's . . .

- bring the bobbin thread to the surface and lock the first stitch
- practice free machine embroidery for several hours (total) before attempting a project
- remember to lower the presser bar lever
- learn to bypass bobbin tension on *your* machine
- move the embroidery hoop smoothly at a moderate speed
- use the correct-sized needle for your fabric and thread

AND DON'TS

- use old, bent, blunt, or scarred needles
- forget to reset tension and stitch length settings each time you sit down to sew
- pull the last stitch away from the needle, as the fabric may pucker (hold the threads)

FLOWER PILLOW

(pictured in Color Plate 5)

The pillow was designed to give you practice in whip stitch with ordinary sewing thread and with silk floss, and in backwards/sidewards/forwards free machine embroidery, as well as calling on the knowledge you already have from Chapters 2 and 3 in crosshatching and satin stitch.

---

you will need:

1 yd. (0,95m) of lavender gingham (I bought 1 yd. of unquilted gingham and ½ yd. (0,50m) of matching quilted gingham for the back)

10″ (25,5cm) square white cotton fabric

2 spools each of gold and one of heavy lime green pure silk twist thread (size D)*

1 spool each of ordinary pink, wine red, bright red, turquoise, purple, kelly green, white, and brown 100% cotton thread

embroidery hoop

darning foot

tracing and graph paper

pencil, ruler, felt-tip pen, tape, pins or spray-on pattern holder

doodle cloths for both white and gingham fabric

pillow form 14″ (35,5cm) x 14″

step-by-step:

1 Place graph paper over the cartoon and trace the design. Number the squares as described in Chapter 1 on blowing up designs, and transfer to full size, drawing with a felt-tip pen. Be sure to let the ink dry before the next step, so you won't smudge the back of your fabric. (Diagram 32)

2 Tape the graph paper to a window, and position and tape the white fabric over it. Copy the flower circles only with a pencil or tailor's chalk. (Note: Transfer the design any way you like; this is my favorite way.)

*Using silk floss requires this pillow be drycleaned.

3 Wind all of your cotton sewing threads onto separate bobbin spools.

4 Prepare your machine for free machine embroidery—lower feed dogs (optional), put on darning foot, set stitch length at 0.

5 Load pink thread on the top and purple into the bobbin, bypassing the bobbin tension in whatever way your machine does it. Turn the upper tension to 9 or the tightest tension.

6 Cut a doodle cloth of white fabric, big enough to stretch over your embroidery hoop. Lay the top of the

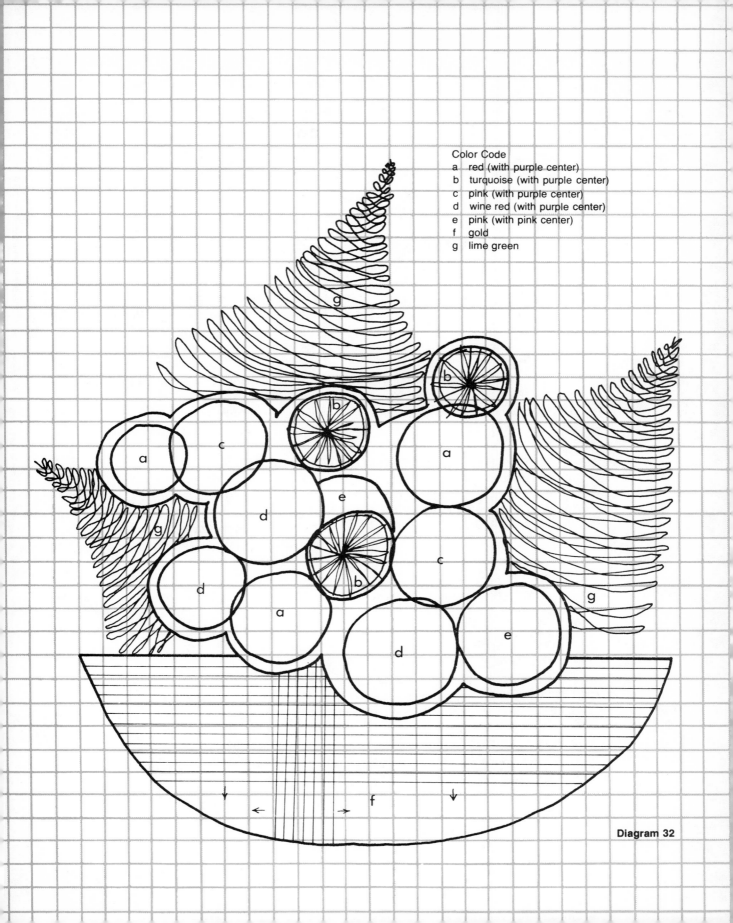

Color Code
a red (with purple center)
b turquoise (with purple center)
c pink (with purple center)
d wine red (with purple center)
e pink (with pink center)
f gold
g lime green

Diagram 32

hoop on a flat surface, put the fabric over it, and press the bottom of the hoop firmly onto the fabric as described in the text above.

7 Practice stitching the purple thread in whip stitch spirals, to be the center of flowers. Remember to lower the presser bar lever and to bring up and lock the bobbin thread for the first stitch. If an upper tension of 9 is not right for your machine, fiddle until you are satisfied—and keep track of your changes by writing notes directly on the doodle cloth.

8 Put white fabric on your embroidery hoop and whip stitch the centers of the red, wine red, and pink flowers. Tie off each thread before starting another flower.

9 Change bobbin threads and stitch the loops on the petals of the wine red, red, and pink flowers.

10 On the underside of the fabric, press lightly with an iron set to cotton.

11 Put white thread in both upper and lower and change the tension and stitch length settings for satin stitch. Because my white fabric is lightweight, I loosened both my upper and lower tensions slightly, until the fabric of the doodle cloth did not pucker.

12 Stitch around the flower shapes in a narrow satin stitch, being careful not to stretch the fabric out of shape on the bias. Cut out the flowers close to the satin stitch.

13 Cut the gingham fabric into a 16″ (40,5cm) square (1″ [2,5cm] on each side of the 14″ [35,5cm] x 14″ pillow for seams). Tape the tracing paper to a window and place the gingham fabric over it, tracing the design of the bowl and ferns onto it with a white pencil or tailor's chalk.

14 Load brown cotton thread into the bobbin and gold pure silk twist (in the heavier weight—size D) on the top. Change the needle to size 14 (90). Put the presser foot back on and set the stitch length to normal (3 on my machine, 10-12 on others).

15 Check tension on the gingham doodle cloth. My upper setting was 5 and my lower slightly loosened.

16 Outline the bowl shape (no need to use hoop) and then fill it in by crosshatching (see Chapter 2). Doesn't that silk feel good while you're working on it!

17 Pin-baste the white flower fabric to the gingham as shown on the design, with the two flowers in the lower right overlapping the bowl.

18 Change the needle size back to 12 (80). Load white thread onto the machine, universal tension, and stitch immediately inside the satin stitch.

19 Back to free machine embroidery again, but not whip stitch—load turquoise into both the bobbin and the top, universal tension. Take off the presser foot, put on the darning foot, and set the stitch length to 0. Load the gingham fabric with appliquéd flowers into the embroidery hoop, and don't worry about the edge of the hoop falling on the stitching of the bowl—it can't hurt it.

20 Stitch the three turquoise flowers in a starburst fashion, back and forth from the center, remembering to lower the presser bar lever and to pull up and lock the bobbin thread for the first stitch. After finishing each flower, cut threads and tie off.

21 Load heavy lime green pure silk twist on the top, and ordinary cotton kelly green into the bobbin, bypassing bobbin tension and resetting top tension to 9 (or whatever worked for whip stitch). Change the needle size to 14 (90).

22 Reposition the hoop to work the whip stitch ferns and start at the top, swinging to the edges of the fern, back to the center, down to the next frond, and out to the edges. Don't worry about following the exact lines of the design, and whistle while you work.

23. Press lightly and finish pillow construction. And don't forget to change the needle back to a 12 (80).

SUMMARY OF TECHNIQUES

| | stitch | | tensions | | | | |
	width	length	top	bobbin	foot	feed dog	comments
free machine embroidery	0	0	loosen	normal	darning	lower	use hoop
couching (free machine)	0	0	normal	loosen	darning	lower	
whip stitch	0	0	tighten	bypass	darning	lower	use hoop

ADDITIONAL IDEAS

■ Use this chapter's flower design on a handbag, purse or tote bag.

■ Write a child's name in free-machined block letters on the yoke of a dress.

■ Work radiating circles of whip stitch flowers from the center out on a tablecloth.

■ Make fabric placecards by free machine embroidering guests' names on non-frayable fabric (like interfacing), cutting out with pinking shears and glueing to colored cardboard.

■ Fill in the letters of "March" for your fabric calendar with free machine scribbling in rainbow colors. Outline them in bold couched thread. (See Chapter 2—Additional Ideas, if you're confused.)

FIVE
MORE FREE MACHINE EMBROIDERY

GLOSSARY

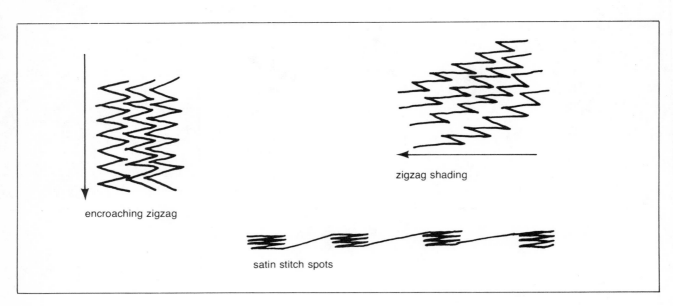

encroaching zigzag

zigzag shading

satin stitch spots

THE TECHNIQUE

In this chapter, we will further explore the possibilities of free machine embroidery, working with and without a hoop. You might as well stash your normal presser foot for the rest of the chapter, as we will keep the darning foot on the whole time.

Whenever possible, use a hoop in free machine embroidery—your work will be neater and more professional looking. But it is important to know how to stitch without a hoop. Why would you want to work without a hoop? Sometimes the design is long and continuous, so that constantly moving the hoop is tedious (as in the Mexican peasant blouse in Chapter 6).

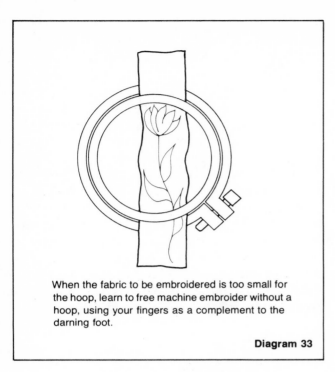

When the fabric to be embroidered is too small for the hoop, learn to free machine embroider without a hoop, using your fingers as a complement to the darning foot.

Diagram 33

Sometimes you have no choice: perhaps the fabric is delicate and will be marred by the impressions left by a hoop, or your piece of fabric is not large enough for a hoop. For example, I once made a spur-of-the-moment present for a friend of one machine embroidered long-stemmed rose, stitched on a long rectangle of fabric too skinny to put into a hoop. (Diagram 33)

For such times, you must learn to use your fingers as a complement to the darning foot, holding the fabric against the needle plate each time the needle enters the fabric. When you are working without a hoop, hold your hands so that the fabric is pressed against the needle plate. (Diagram 34)

You can see that if you held your fingers under the fabric, you might lift the fabric away from the needleplate, so that stitches are not formed. When you are not working with a hoop, it is important to sew slowly and smoothly in order to give yourself plenty of time to readjust your grasp on the fabric. To keep a large piece of cloth from unrolling each time you change grasps, roll up the excess fabric and secure it with clothespins.

Your preparations for free machine embroidery without a hoop are the same as for with a hoop—stitch length 0, stitch width whatever you want, covering or lowering feed dogs optional, darning foot on. You will need a flat surface to support the fabric, so if you have a free-arm machine, add whatever is needed to make it flat (e.g., the carrying case of my machine becomes a flat sewing surface when added to the free arm).

Tensions are quite important, and as always, check the conditions on a doodle cloth before attempting a finished article. To prevent puckers, I almost automatically loosen both top and bobbin tensions for all free machine embroidery.

Always, always, bring up the bobbin thread (see Chapter 4), lower the presser foot, and take about three stitches in one place to lock the first stitch. Cut off thread ends.

My machine has a variable-speed foot pedal and I like to put it on Slow for free machine stitching without a

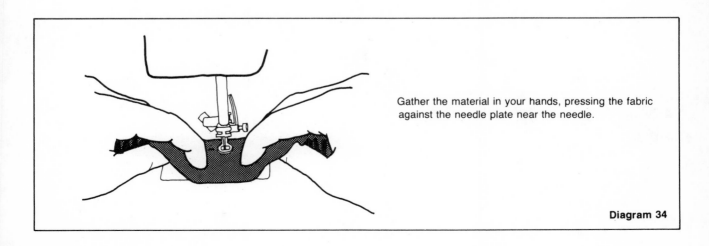

Gather the material in your hands, pressing the fabric against the needle plate near the needle.

Diagram 34

hoop. When you see curves, corners, or spirals approaching the needle, slow down and use your fingers to hold the material against the plate for each stitch —these are the situations that will pucker your fabric if you are not careful.

After you finish the design, always press it on the underside to remove any tendency toward puckers.

Knowing how to free machine embroider without a hoop comes in handy on large items, like quilts. Often you will need help simply to maneuver the enormous bulk of fabric under the needle. I know an artist who has developed a very efficient quilt-moving machine: four children, who support the corners of the quilt, and run from side to side in a hilarious choreography as their mother stitches and screams commands.

Now that you know how to work without a hoop, let's explore some more effects possible with free machine embroidery.

All you people with straight stitch machines, don't despair at your zigzagless world—there is an easy way to fill in areas of color that does not require a zigzag. Draw your design on the right side of the fabric and back the whole thing with organza, interfacing, or typing paper. Stretch the fabric in a hoop. Set up the machine for free machine embroidery—darning foot, 0 stitch length, universal tension, cotton sewing machine thread in upper and lower. Now take a piece of any thick thread—crochet cotton, needlepoint yarn, knitting wool, embroidery floss—and lay it on the outline of the design. Lower the presser bar lever and hand turn the wheel until the needle is piercing the thick thread and the bobbin thread is brought up. Lock the stitch and cut off the thread ends. Stitch right through the thick thread in small stitches, until the design is solidly filled (Plate 15). You can also stitch back and forth in a manner similar to the long-and-short stitches of hand

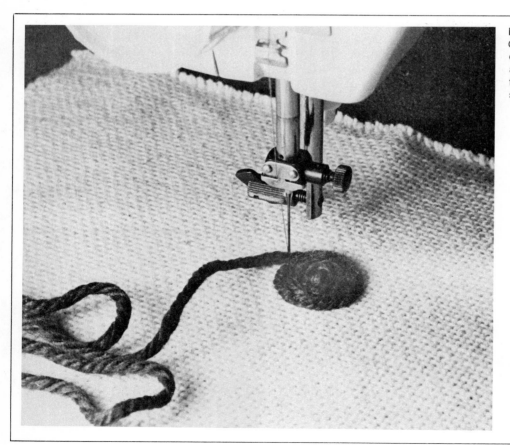

Plate 15
Couching-by-piercing is an easy way to achieve large areas of color and texture fast. Here yarn is being spiralled into a flower form.

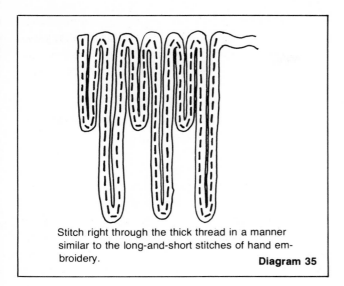

Stitch right through the thick thread in a manner similar to the long-and-short stitches of hand embroidery.

Diagram 35

embroidery (Diagram 35). If your sewing machine thread color matches the thick thread, stitches will be practically invisible.

When you are done stitching, remove the fabric from under the needle. Then thread a tapestry needle with the ends of thick thread still on the surface. Pull these threads to the underside of the fabric and cut them off ¼″ (6mm) from the fabric surface. The ends need no further treatment as your straight stitches have already secured them.

A variation of this couching-by-piercing can be done using invisible nylon thread in the top (see Supply List) and ordinary sewing machine thread in the bobbin. Instead of piercing all of the heavy thread (rug yarn, floss, etc.), only selected parts are held down by the invisible thread, which adds a beautiful texture to your work. Choose a heavyweight backing fabric (such as are found at upholstery and drapery stores) so you won't need a hoop. Set up the machine for free machine embroidery. You will lay down two parallel lines of nylon thread, stitching at the same time by sewing back and forth between the lines, but will only pierce the yarn on each parallel line.

Thus the movement is:

Step 1 Draw two parallel lines on your backing fabric. Start in the middle interval by bringing up the bobbin thread and locking the first stitch.

Step 2 Lay the end of a long piece of yarn on the surface of the fabric from the middle to the left side. Stitch down across the end of the yarn to secure it, and then stitch along the underside of the yarn to the left parallel line *without piercing the yarn*. Stop the needle in the fabric at the parallel line and carefully stitch up over the yarn on the parallel line. (Diagram 36a)

Step 3 Stitch across the right parallel line without

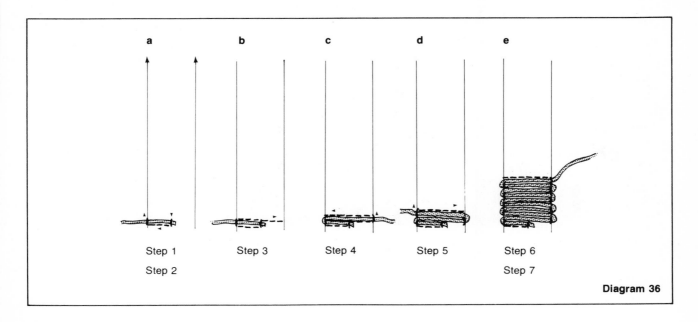

| a | b | c | d | e |

Step 1   Step 3   Step 4   Step 5   Step 6

Step 2   Step 7

Diagram 36

piercing the yarn already laid down. Stop the needle in the fabric at the parallel line. (Diagram 36b)

Step 4 Now pull the yarn across the interval directly *behind* the darning foot and needle. Stitch up over the yarn on the parallel line. (Diagram 36c)

Step 5 Stitch across the interval to the left parallel line, stopping the needle in the fabric on the line. Pull the yarn straight across the interval and stitch up over it. (Diagram 36d)

Step 6 Repeat until finished.

Step 7 Lock and cut off sewing machine threads. Leave a 3″ (7,5cm) tail on the yarn, which is threaded into a tapestry needle, pulled to the back, and cut off. (Diagram 36e)

This method of securing yarn to a surface can also be used in isolated motifs like flower heads. If the item is not a washable garment, the loops at the outside edge can be cut and fuzzed for added texture. Any article that has been stitched with invisible nylon thread should be ironed on the underside with a cool-warm iron.

The technique of filling an area with solid machine satin stitch is called encroaching zigzag. It's one of my favorite techniques, for while it looks incredibly difficult to others, it is really quite easy and fast to work. You often see it used on the front of garments made in India and Mexico.

For the best results in encroaching zigzag, use an extra-fine cotton or rayon sewing machine thread (see Supply List). This is the one situation in which you may want to cover or lower your feed dogs, because the buildup of threads on the back occasionally snags on the teeth of the feed dogs. Otherwise, set up the machine for free machine embroidery as usual—darning foot on, stitch length at 0, stitch width at whatever you like. Since zigzag tends to pull at the fibers of the fabric, I like to back my material with organza. Again, whenever possible, use a hoop to keep the material stretched tight.

To fill in a shape with solid encroaching zigzag, run the machine at a rapid rate, but move the fabric slowly and smoothly. You can either lay down lines of satin stitch that snuggle up to each other, or you can put a third row of satin stitch on top of the first two rows. It is sometimes easier to follow a stitching line if the needle is decentered to the left or right, so you can be sure the needle is entering the fabric exactly where you want it to. (Plate 16)

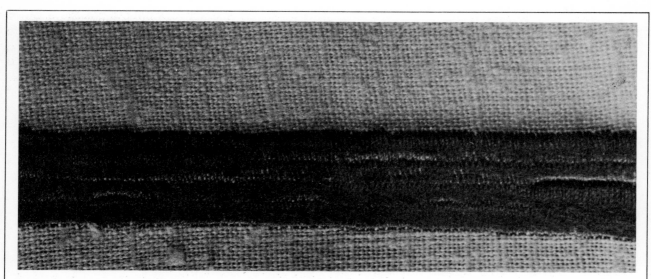

Plate 16 Solid encroaching zigzag can be worked with rows of satin stitch next to each other or a third row of satin stitch worked over two previous rows.

Another way to fill a shape is by subtly shading with zigzag stitches in more of a sidewards motion of the hoop than the up-and-down parallel movements of encroaching zigzag. For this shading, I tighten my bobbin tension slightly, using extra-fine rayon thread in the top and ordinary 100% cotton thread in the bobbin. Because this shading imparts a delicate feeling, I like to use finely woven fabrics like handkerchief linen or lightweight cotton (Plate 17). And since we match the thread to the fabric and the needle to the thread, I then use a Size 10/11 (70) needle. Stitch as if you were climbing stairs, carefully layering your zigzag stitches (Diagram 37). Fill from the widest parts to the narrowest, lapping each row over the previous row. Keep

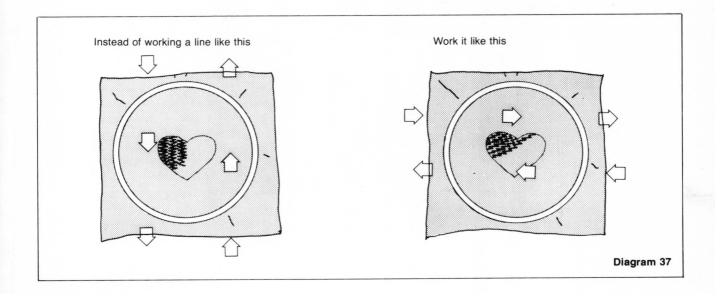

Instead of working a line like this

Work it like this

Diagram 37

Plate 18
Satin stitch spots are worked by making about 10 stitches per knot. (Handkerchief courtesy of Riccar.)

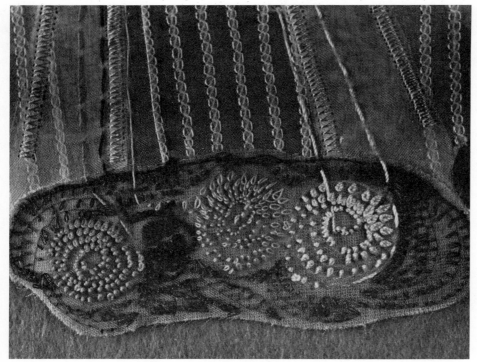

Plate 19
After bonding iron-on interfacing to the back, the top thread is removed to make detached whip stitches.

Do's . . .

- ◼ use a hoop whenever possible
- ◼ learn to use your fingers as a complement to the darning foot
- ◼ decenter the needle to control zigzag exactly

AND DON'TS

- ◼ work whip stitch without a hoop

---

the stitches horizontally parallel and don't turn the hoop around as you stitch. The movement of the hoop is back and forth, edging slowly forward to fill in the shape. If you miss a spot, go back and fill it in.

For a French knot effect, solid zigzag can be done in small spots, with about 10 stitches per knot. If the spots are grouped, one small stitch can be taken between them, without the need to tie off the ends of each spot. If you have a vari-width zigzag dial, satin stitch spots can be made by carefully changing the zigzag width from 0 to the widest stitch and back to 0. For added texture, cut some of the spots with a seam ripper to make tiny tufts of thread. However, don't use this technique on items to be washed unless you bond the back of the satin stitch spots with iron-on interfacing to keep the threads from pulling out. (Plate 18)

Another way to gain unusual texture is to work de-tached whip stitch lines or spirals. Remember whip stitch? (See Chapter 4). Tighten your top tension and completely loosen or bypass the bobbin tension. Be sure the fabric is stretched in a hoop, because whip stitch is particularly pucker-producing. Bring up the bobbin thread and lower the presser bar lever, but don't lock the first stitch (I know, I know, I said ALWAYS, but . . .). Hold the threads securely as you start a line of whip stitch. When you finish, raise the presser foot and pull the hoop gently to the side away from the needle. Cut off the threads, leaving ends a few inches long. Remove the hoop and press the fabric from the back. Now bond iron-on interfacing to the back. Turn the fabric to the right side, and with tweezers or a blunt tapestry needle, gently pull out the top thread, as if you were removing a basting thread. Beautiful loops of thread are left. (Plate 19)

THE PROJECT

ℬREAD BOARD APRON

(pictured in Color Plate 2)

The apron challenges your new skills in whip stitch, zigzag shading, satin stitch spots, and couching-by-piercing. It also shows you how to deal with a difficult fabric with a rippled surface.

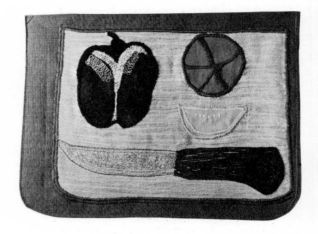

you will need:

1⅞ yds. (1,75m) for a woman, 2⅛ yds. (1,95m) for a man, of mustard-colored fabric

10″ (25,5cm)-square piece of off-white, Indian-look fabric (plus extra for a doodle cloth), and a 10″ (25,5cm)-square piece of rust-colored fabric

scraps of green, yellow, and red fabric

white organza

extra-fine cotton threads in white, green, red, yellow, gray, light and dark blue, brown, and rust

brown crochet cotton

doodle cloth of Indian-look fabric

scissors, tissue paper, felt-tip pen, pins or spray-on pattern holder, embroidery hoop

pattern for an apron

step-by-step:

1 Trace the cartoons for the green pepper, tomato, and lemon onto scraps of green, red, and yellow fabric respectively. (Diagram 38)

2 Load the machine with white extra-fine cotton thread on top and white on the bobbin. Set up the machine for free machine embroidery: stitch length 0, stitch width to a wide zigzag, darning foot on, feed dogs covered or lowered (optional), slightly loosened upper tension.

3 Put the green fabric into a hoop and back it with typing paper. Fill in the white zigzag shading area (see cartoon).

4 Change the stitch width to 0, tighten top tension, and loosen bobbin tension. Do whip stitch in a figure 8, running the machine at a fast rate but moving the hoop slowly, to produce the chalky seed area.

5 Take the fabric out of the hoop and gently tear off the typing paper. Always press from the underside. Place a towel on the ironing board to cushion stitches and prevent flattening. (You will work the green pepper outline later.)

6 Reset the machine for free machine zigzag: bobbin tension normal, top tension slightly loosened, stitch width wide zigzag. Load red extra-fine rayon thread into the top and don't change the bobbin.

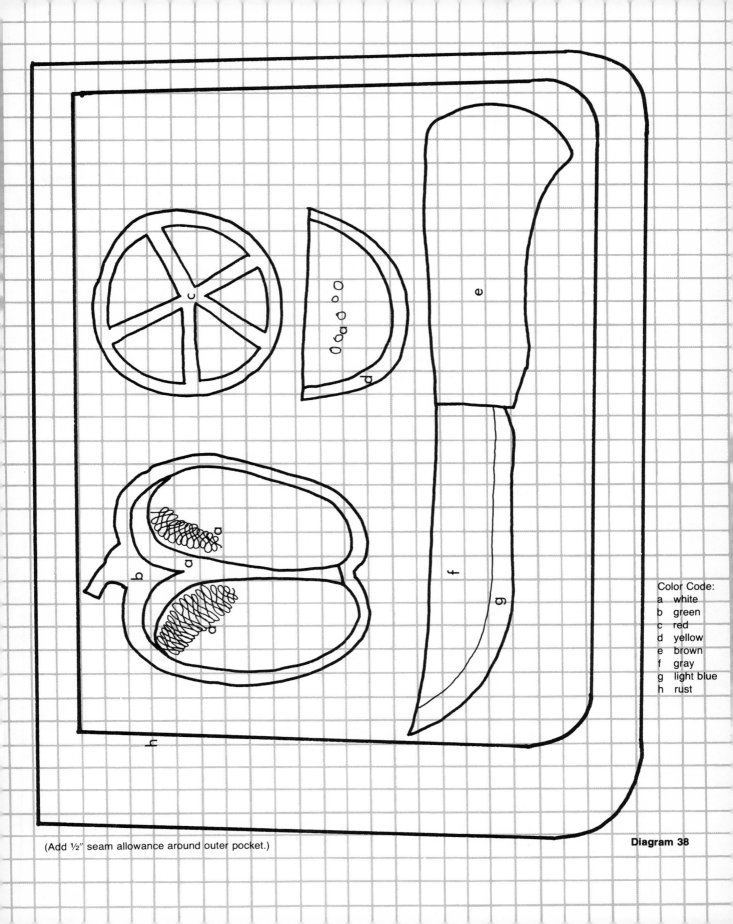

(Add ½″ seam allowance around outer pocket.)

Color Code:
a white
b green
c red
d yellow
e brown
f gray
g light blue
h rust

Diagram 38

7 Put the red fabric into the hoop, back it with typing paper, and work the center pulp in lines of encroaching zigzag. Take the fabric out of the hoop and gently tear off the typing paper. Press. (You will work the red outline later.)

8 Put the off-white, Indian-look fabric over the cartoon and trace the design lightly with a pencil.

9 Cut out the red tomato and pin it in position on the off-white fabric. Place this in the hoop and back it with typing paper. Satin stitch the edge of the tomato with the red rayon thread to the off-white fabric. Gently tear off the typing paper. Remove hoop and press.

10 Cut out the lemon wedge and pin it in position on the off-white fabric. Place this in the hoop and back it with typing paper. Load the machine with white extra-fine thread on top and satin stitch the white rind on the lemon wedge, starting at the right side. Make the satin stitch spots, or seeds, by taking about ten stitches in one place and then moving ahead one zigzag stitch for another seed.

11 Load yellow extra-fine rayon thread into the top and satin stitch the remaining edge of the lemon. Gently tear the paper off the back and remove the fabric from the hoop. Press.

12 Place the white organza over the cartoon and copy the knife outline with pencil. Put the organza into a hoop so that the knife end shows, and back it with typing paper.

13 Load gray extra-fine rayon thread into the top and fill the inner part of the knife with zigzag shading, starting at the handle end and ending with the tapered point. Remove from the hoop and press.

14 Load the top with brown thread (or invisible nylon, if you wish). Lay the partially worked organza in place on the off-white fabric, press, and back with typing paper.

15 Lay the end of a ball of brown crochet cotton along the outline of the knife. Bring up the bobbin thread and lock it. Couch the brown crochet cotton to the organza by either piercing the heavy thread or using a narrow zigzag. Continue to couch the brown crochet cotton in one continuous line until you fill the entire knife handle shape. Thread a tapestry needle and pull both beginning and ending threads through to the back. Cut them—do not knot as it would make a bump. The zigzag stitches will hold the thread in place.

16 Load the machine with light blue extra-fine rayon and satin stitch the remaining edge of the knife.

SUMMARY OF TECHNIQUES

	stitch		tensions				
	width	length	top	bobbin	foot	feed dog	comments
free machine quilting	0	0	loosen	normal	darning	lower	no hoop
couching-by-piercing	0	0	universal		darning	lower	use heavy backing fabric
encroaching (zz)	1–4	0	loosen	normal	darning	lower	use extra-fine thread
zigzag shading	1–4	0	loosen	tighten	darning	lower	use extra-fine thread
satin stitch spots	1–4	0	loosen	normal	darning	lower	about 10 stitches/spot
detached whip stitch	0	0	tighten	bypass	darning	lower	bond with iron-on interfacing and remove top thread

17 Cut the organza close to the outline of the knife. Gently tear away the typing paper and press from the underside (if you used nylon thread, use a cool-warm iron). Reload the machine with dark blue extra-fine thread and outline the knife blade with straight stitch.

18 Cut out the rust-colored apron pocket.

19 Cut out the outline of the off-white fabric and pin into place on the pocket, backing it with typing paper. Load the machine with rust extra-fine thread and satin stitch the off-white fabric to the pocket. Run a second row of satin stitch on the left side and bottom to increase the feeling of a three-dimensional bread board.

20 Press under seam allowances and top fold of pocket. Stitch into place on the apron.

21 Finish apron construction.

ADDITIONAL IDEAS

■ Work this chapter's design as a kitchen wallhanging by padding and free machine quilting it.

■ Decorate a monkscloth lampshade with couched wool Mexican motifs (see page 186, Bibliography) by piercing the wool.

■ Use solid lines of zigzag shading on a decorative pillow to give the feeling of dawn.

■ Work detached whip stitch and satin stitch spots on wool in small circles, then cut out and make covered buttons of the circles.

■ Draw "April" on your fabric calendar, surrounded by Easter eggs, a basket, and a bunny, all worked in solid encroaching zigzag in pastel colors. (See Chapter 2—Additional Ideas, if you missed out.)

SIX
Heavy THREADS IN BOBBIN

GLOSSARY

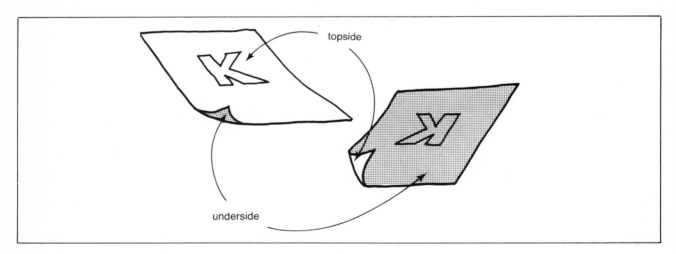

topside

underside

THE TECHNIQUE

Now that you have mastered free machine embroidery with and without a hoop, you are ready to branch out into one of the most spectacular forms of decorative machine stitchery—laying thick threads onto the surface of your work to create texture. But how to thread that fat fiber through the needle? The secret: you *don't* thread it through the needle. Instead you load it into the

bobbin case and stitch with the underside of your garment up, thereby laying the thread on the surface of your material when you turn it over. (Diagram 39)

How thick can the thread be? The thickest I've tried is four-ply knitting yarn, but since not much can be wound onto the bobbin at a time, which means reloading several times per project, I've been too lazy to experiment further. Otherwise, I've wound up to six strands of embroidery floss, pearl cotton, linen warp,

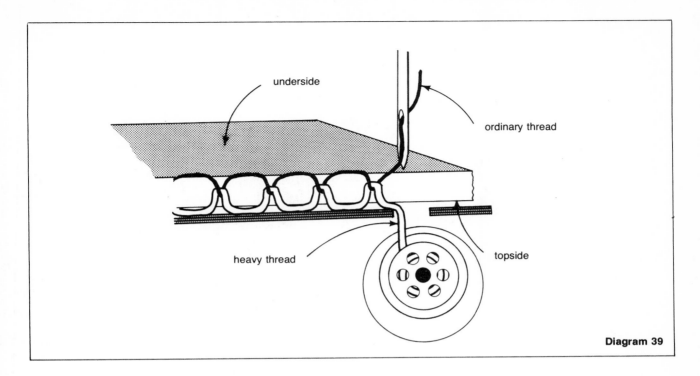

underside

ordinary thread

heavy thread

topside

Diagram 39

slubby yarns, raffia, and my own combinations of yarns (a strand of gold with a strand of crochet cotton, for example).

In order to allow these thick threads to pass through your bobbin case without breaking, which they would if they passed through the ordinary bobbin tension spring, you must determine how to bypass bobbin tension on your machine. Look at the chart in Chapter 4 to find your machine's adaptation. Remember that if you must loosen a screw to release the bobbin tension, place a piece of felt or other soft material under the bobbin case on the table to prevent the screw from falling out, bouncing off the table, and hiding itself in far corners.

To wind thick threads onto your bobbin, set up your machine for winding bobbins the way you normally would (i.e., disengage the flywheel, put the empty bobbin wherever it goes for winding). If the thread comes on a small cardboard tube and isn't too thick, you can place the tube on the upper thread holder, wind the thread around one thread guide into the empty bobbin, and slowly fill the bobbin, keeping one

hand on the spool of thread to keep it from flying off, and one on the thread near the bobbin to help it feed evenly. If the spool of thread is quite large, put a pencil through the center of the spool or cone of thick thread and hold it in your right hand. Put the end of the thread through the hole in your bobbin, just as you would to wind ordinary machine thread. Hand turn the bobbin several times until the thread end is secured and then use the fingers of your left hand to guide the thread evenly onto the bobbin. Don't drive the machine too fast or the thread may jump the bobbin and wind itself into a horrible mess around the bobbin shaft (Diagram 40). For some threads (embroidery floss, very thick wool, etc.), you will have to hand wind the bobbins. Be careful not to pull too tightly as you patiently wind on the thread. Also, don't wind the bobbins too full or they will not fit into the bobbin case.

If you have a brand that winds the bobbin in the machine, use a Size 16 needle. The large eye will accommodate such heavy threads as metallic, crochet cotton, and darning wools. Use the secondary spool holder to hold the heavy thread cones, balls, or spools.

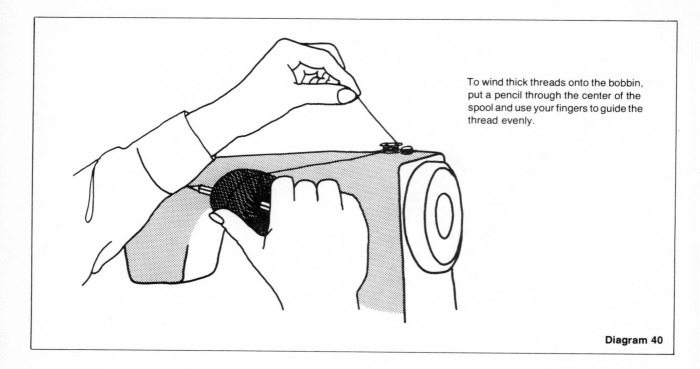

To wind thick threads onto the bobbin, put a pencil through the center of the spool and use your fingers to guide the thread evenly.

Diagram 40

You can hand wind heavier threads and loosen bobbin tension on your second purchased bobbin case, but you cannot bypass bobbin tension on these machines.

Since your heavy bobbin thread cannot pass easily through ordinary cottons and other medium-to-tightly-woven fabrics, the upper tension should be loosened somewhat (still loosening or bypassing bobbin tension and working from the underside), allowing the bobbin thread to lie on the surface of the material, similar to couching in hand embroidery.

I cannot emphasize enough the importance of a doodle cloth in using thick threads. In the Mexican peasant blouse project for this chapter, I used a heavy 100% polyester Swedish thread found in many fabric stores. It was definitely too thick to pass through the needle, so I assumed that I would need to bypass bobbin tension and to loosen the upper tension; however doing so produced an unpleasant, irregular, wavy effect when what I wanted was a straight couched line (perhaps another time I may use that wavy effect to advantage). I ended up using a normal bobbin tension setting and a very tight upper tension.

Of course, when I put the lines of blue thread onto the yoke of the blouse, I was stitching through both the fabric and the interfacing, so my doodle cloth was also a piece of fabric with interfacing. But when I stitched three lines of blue onto the sleeve, I had to set up a new doodle cloth, double-folded to simulate the hem in the sleeve—and it's a good thing I did, because the tension that was right for fabric with interfacing was all wrong for doubled fabric.

For ordinary straight stitch, you need only load the bobbin with the thick thread, loosen or bypass bobbin tension, loosen the upper tension slightly, and stitch from the underside with the presser foot on, just as you would for everyday seam sewing. Fanatics stitch in the same direction for every row of thread, including basting, to prevent puckering. At any rate, do keep track as you work, checking to see that all is going well. Since you're working from the underside, you are more apt to make mistakes than you would if you could see what was happening to your threads.

Speaking of mistakes, for the Mexican peasant blouse, I stitched everything else first, leaving the two lines of couching closest to the neck edge and the yoke seam to serve as final topstitching. By the time I had finished assembling the garment and was ready to add those last two lines of stitching, I thought I knew everything—and proceeded to bypass bobbin tension when I loaded the heavy thread into the machine. I stitched a ways before discovering I was producing that irregular wavy line I didn't want and had to rip out a long line of stitching (grumble). I should have consulted my doodle cloth for the correct settings.

If the bobbin thread is too thick to draw up through your material and lock, be sure you hold both threads as you take the first few stitches. Otherwise, you can end up with an incredible snafu in the bobbin case.

By using buttonhole thread on the upper and a Size 14 or 16 (90-100) needle, again working from the underside with heavy thread bypassing bobbin tension, a loopy, heavily textured effect called cable stitch can be made. The large needle also allows you to pull up and lock the first stitch. Move the work slowly so that the bobbin thread has a chance to loop. (Plate 20)

I am not offering specific directions to loosen or tighten top tension because it varies according to the type and weight of thread you use. Experiment on a

Plate 20 On the top, knitting yarn has been handwound onto the bobbin and bobbin tension bypassed to make a cable stitch. In the middle, pearl cotton has been worked with the same tension settings, which do not produce cable stitch without further experimentation. On the bottom, the top thread has pulled to the side of the knotting yarn in large loops.

doodle cloth and remember that of the top and bobbin thread weights, the heavier thread will pull the lighter thread; therefore, if you want the bobbin thread to loop, don't use a top thread heavier than it. The character of the bobbin thread will also affect the look of the cable stitch—for example, embroidery floss loops more than linen.

Naturally you can load thick thread in the bobbin, work from the underside of the fabric, and do free machine embroidery with a darning foot and no hoop. Don't worry too much about regularity when you are curling, looping, and spiraling around the material. Part of the charm of this kind of machine stitchery is its spontaneity and free formation.

A simple yet exquisite effect can be produced by winding thick gold thread (available in most fabric stores in many weights) onto the bobbin, setting up the machine for free machine embroidery, bypassing bobbin tension, working from the underside, and making spirals and curlicues on the borders of luxurious fabrics like velvet, velveteen, crêpe (which should be backed by typing paper while working), silk, and satin. (Plate 21)

Because of the use of metallic threads, be careful to wash the garment with cold water, and don't rub it or use chemicals. If you want any garment machine washable, you should not incorporate wool, silk floss, or other nonwashable threads into the design.

Plate 21
Gold thread worked from the underside on velvet can look elegant.

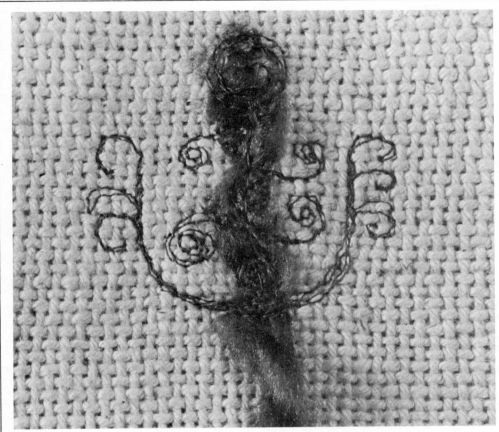

Plate 22
Secure thick threads onto the surface of a fabric with free machine embroidery.

Starting and ending these thick threads on garments can be messy. I recommend pulling the fat thread through to the back and tying off, but sometimes knots do not hold well, so tie a double knot and secure it with fabric glue.

What materials are appropriate for embellishment from the underside? Cotton, wool, knits—almost any are easy to work with except those with high naps like fake fur or exaggerated puckers like seersucker or the Indian-look fabrics. Just remember that if you want to do free machine embroidery with a heavy thread in the bobbin and without a hoop, as is done in the project for this chapter, either your fabric must be heavy enough not to pucker, or it must be backed with interfacing or typing paper, as is the yoke in the Mexican peasant blouse.

Of course, if your fabric is loosely woven, like burlap or hopsacking, you can set up the machine for free machine embroidery, bypass bobbin tension, work from the *topside,* and bring those unusual fibers to the surface of your work in trailing loops or whip stitch spirals (see Chapter 4). Whenever possible, though, I would use a hoop when doing whip stitch as it tends to pull the fabric badly.

Also, if you're too lazy to hand wind these fat fibers into the bobbin, you can always lay them onto the surface of your fabric and free machine stitch over them with regular thread, setting your machine up for free machine embroidery without a hoop, using the darning foot. You can either stitch freely back and forth over the heavy thread, use your zigzag or decorative stitches, or be fancy with spirals and loops. (Plate 22)

Do's . . .

- experiment on a doodle cloth first
- hold ends of both threads as you begin to stitch
- try stitching everything—ribbon, string, bread bags, wire, straw, raffia, fishing line, etc.
- reset the tension and other settings to normal at the end of a project

AND DON'TS

- wind bobbins too full of heavy threads or they won't fit into the case

You can also completely cover a cord or thick yarn with satin stitch, twisting soft yarns to keep them from being flattened. In this case, loosen top tension and use a cording foot.

What styles of clothing are amenable to decoration with thick yarns? If you are stitching in straight lines from the underside, the contours of almost any pattern can be followed; but if you are working free machine embroidery without a hoop from the underside, it is easier to work near the edge of the garment, so that you can more easily grasp and maneuver the material—look for yokes, cummerbunds, borders, small purses, headbands, etc., to decorate.

EXICAN PEASANT BLOUSE

(pictured in Color Plate 3)

This blouse draws on your understanding of free machine embroidery without a hoop, using the darning foot, and of winding thicker threads onto the bobbin, to be stitched from the underside in both free machine embroidery and straight stitch with a presser foot. While it looks complicated, it isn't–I finished the front yoke in half an hour.

you will need:

pattern and yardage for a blouse with a square yoke at least 2¼″ (5,6cm) wide

three colors of washable blue thick thread (I used 100% polyester; pearl cotton that is colorfast could also be used): dark, medium, and light blue

one spool of bronze sewing machine thread (I used Spanish rayon with a sheen that gives the design an extra oomph)

one spool of dark blue ordinary 100% cotton

interfacing

tissue paper, pencil, pins, scissors,

Note: To avoid confusion, I code the thick blue bobbin threads with an H for heavy and call the dark blue 100% cotton thread "ordinary thread." The wrong side of the garment is called "underside" and the outer side, "topside."

step-by-step:

1 Place the tissue paper over the part of the design to be done in bronze thread and copy the cartoon with a felt-tip pen. Fold your tissue paper exactly in half as indicated, and copy the second half of the design, which is a mirror image of the first half. Just for fun, try to draw the design without lifting your pen from the page, retracing lines when necessary, which is what you will later do with the needle of your machine. (Diagram 41 and 42)

2 Cut away excess tissue paper from the front and back yoke pattern pieces, and pin to your fabric. On the white fabric, trace around each yoke with a pencil. Cut out the yokes in two large rectangles, leaving wide margins (at least 2″ or 5cm) all around, and not cutting into the square of the neck area. This is to make the stitching easier for you.

3 Baste interfacing to the back of each yoke. Baste along the ⅝″ (1,5cm) seam line. Since you are working from the underside, this basted line will be used as a spacing guideline when you begin stitching.

4 Cut a rectangle of doodle cloth and back it with interfacing.

5 Wind three separate bobbins of the three shades of heavy (H) blue thread.

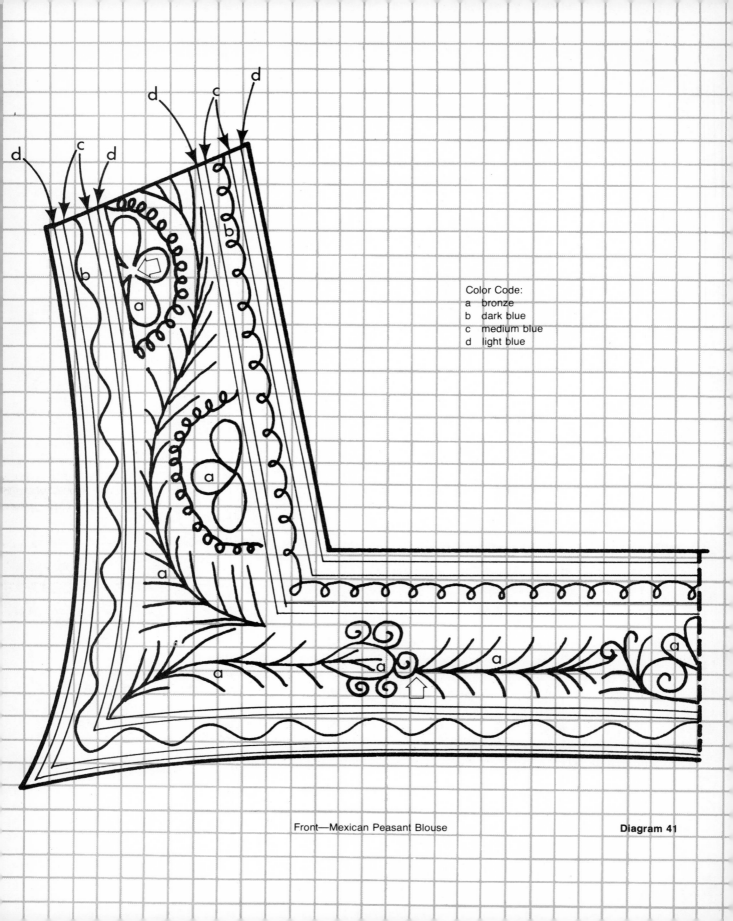

Color Code:
a bronze
b dark blue
c medium blue
d light blue

Front—Mexican Peasant Blouse   **Diagram 41**

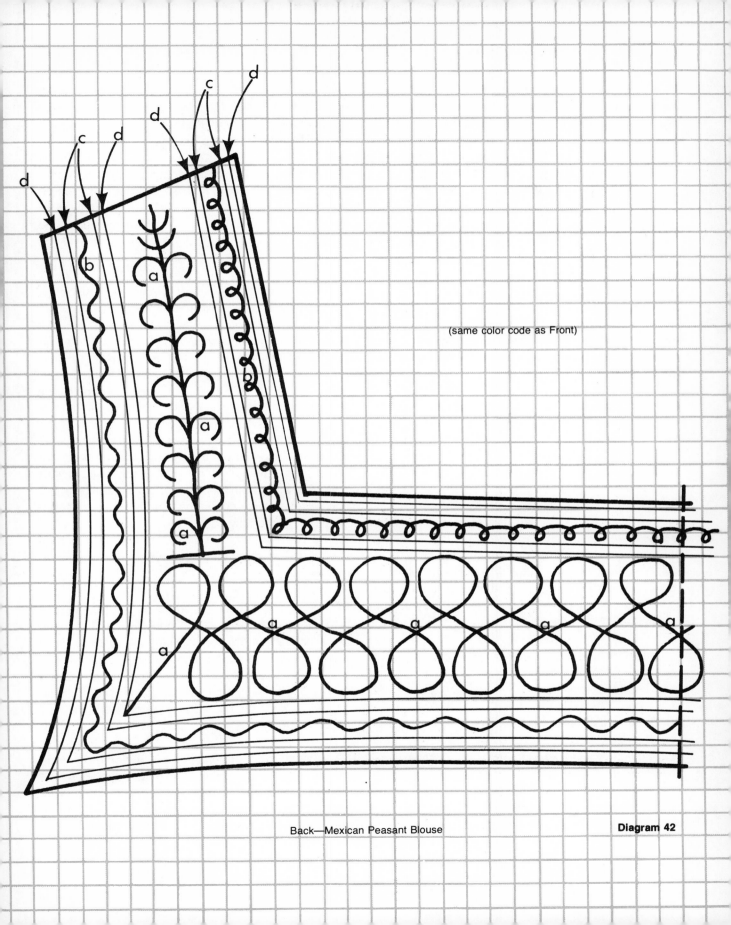

(same color code as Front)

Back—Mexican Peasant Blouse

Diagram 42

6 Set up your machine for straight stitch with heavy thread in the bobbin, worked from the underside—i.e., set the stitch length for slightly longer than a normal seam (3 or 10-12), load the top with the dark blue ordinary 100% cotton, load the bobbin with the medium blue (H), leave on the presser foot.

7 Determine on your doodle cloth the best tension settings and make a note of these. I used a normal lower tension (remember, bypassing tension produced an unwanted wavy line on my machine) and the tightest upper tension.

8 On the underside of the front yoke, stitch a straight line ⅛″ (3mm) from edge seam line along the right sleeve, turning a corner, along the bottom of the yoke to the opposite corner, up the left sleeve, and off the fabric. Repeat for the back yoke.

9 On the underside of both front and back yokes, stitch another medium-blue (H) line ¼″ (6mm) away from the line you just finished.

10 Now do the same at the neck edge, stitching from the underside.

11 Leave in the top thread, but change the bobbin thread to light blue (H). You will not stitch the line of light blue at the neck and yoke seam at this time, doing it as topstitching later. Stitch a line of light blue (H) thread from the underside, ⅛″ (3mm) from the innermost medium blue (H) lines, at both the lower yoke and neck sides of the blouse.

12 Load dark blue (H) thread into the bobbin and put on the darning foot. Change the stitch length to 0 (cover the feed dogs—optional).

13 Starting at the underside of the right front shoulder with the neck edge of the yoke pointing at your belly, move the fabric in small counterclockwise loops, working from left to right as if you were practicing penmanship lessons in the letter "e." Make a loop at the corner of the yoke and turn the fabric so the neck edge is now pointing at you; likewise at the opposite corner. These

dark blue (H) free-form e's fall in the ¼″ (6mm) width between the medium blue (H) lines. Don't worry about regularity—the flowing freeness of these loops is charming. Repeat on the back yoke.

14 On the underside of the right front shoulder edge, between the remaining two lines of medium blue (H) stitching, stitch a free-form wavy line. I prefer to stitch top to bottom, but you may prefer to turn the neck edge toward you again and stitch from left to right, as if you were writing. Repeat for back yoke.

15 Have a cup of coffee. Stretch your neck muscles—you'll need to be relaxed for the next part.

16 Load extra-fine bronze thread into the top and bottom. Fiddle on your doodle cloth until you have a tension that pulls the top thread slightly to the underside (I tightened my bobbin one notch and kept the top at 5, or normal tension). Ready for some fun?

17 Pin the tissue paper design onto the front yoke, centering the design in the space between the inner lines of light blue (H) stitching. If the front band of your pattern is wider than this design, cut the design at the flowers (as shown), center the middle part on your front yoke, move the flowers and side design to the outer edges of your yoke, and plan to add some more spokes to the tendrils at the center (see arrows on cartoon).

18 Pull up the bobbin thread, lower the presser bar lever, and lock the first stitch. Then free machine baste the main lines of the design onto the topside of your yoke, stitching right through the tissue paper, but avoiding pins. Unless you are not sure of yourself, you do not need to stitch every little tendril and curlicue, instead filling in spontaneously as you stitch. Tear off tissue paper.

19 Working from the topside now and starting at the center of the three blobs on the right shoulder (see arrow on cartoon), fill in the design. Remember to work smoothly, not too fast, and to work over each line at least twice. The tendrils are worked by stitching to the

SUMMARY OF TECHNIQUES

| | stitch | | tensions | | | | |
	width	length	top	bobbin	foot	feed dog	comments
couching heavy threads	0–4	10–12	loosen	bypass	presser	in place	from the underside
cable stitch	0	0	varies	bypass	darning	lower	large-eye needle and heavey thread on top

end of a line, stitching around in an oval three or four times, and then stitching back to the main stalk. You can't help but pat yourself on the back when you finish this exciting part.

20 Work the back in the same manner. If you wish, you may repeat the front yoke design on the back; otherwise use the simple design on page 81.

21 Before finishing garment construction, turn up and press in the sleeve and bottom hems—it is easier to work with the fabric flat. If your pattern calls for a deeper sleeve hem than 1″ (2,5cm), cut off all excess. Turn all hems under ½″ (1,3cm).

22 Load light blue (H) into the bobbin and ordinary dark blue onto the top. Change your tension setting and stitch length to whatever you used in Step 7. Put the presser foot back on.

23 On the underside of the sleeve (same as you did around the yoke), stitch three lines of blue (H) thread ⅛″ (3mm) apart, with the lightest color at the bottom of the sleeve hem. On the underside of the bottom hem, stitch three lines of blue (H) thread ⅛″ (3mm) apart, starting with a line of light blue (H) thread ⅛″ (3mm) away from the turned edge of the bottom hem, and ending with the darkest blue (H) nearest the bottom of the hem.

24 Change tension settings and finish garment construction, matching lines of stitching at shoulder, undersleeve, and side seams. Do not topstitch yoke yet.

25 Reload light blue (H) into the bobbin, ordinary dark blue on top, and change tension settings, as in Step 22.

26 For topstitching, work from the underside of the yoke, stitching a straight seam ⅛″ (3mm) from the neck edge. Stitch another seam ⅛″ (3mm) away from the lower yoke.

27 Press and celebrate—you're done!

ADDITIONAL IDEAS

■ Use this chapter's design for a border on place mats.

■ Emphasize the outline of a shaped valance with lines of heavy thread worked from the underside.

■ Decorate the neck and sleeve edge of a velveteen caftan from the underside with swirls of gold thread.

■ Make a cover for a wastebasket, working some lines of heavy thread from the underside and some loopy bouclé-like threads from the topside.

■ Wind crochet cotton in crocus colors onto bobbins and fill in the letters of "May" for your fabric calendar, working from the underside. (Still confused? See Chapter 2—Additional Ideas.)

SEVEN

AUTOMATIC STITCHES

GLOSSARY

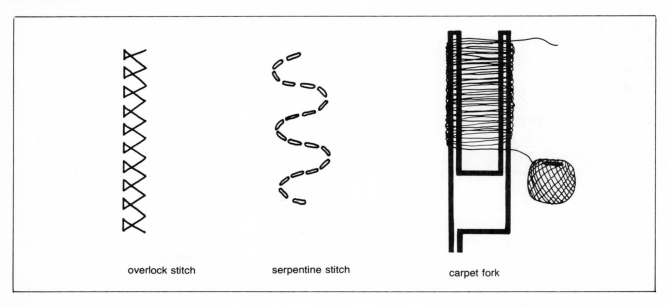

overlock stitch   serpentine stitch   carpet fork

THE TECHNIQUE

The ability of some machines to make automatic stitches greatly extends the range of decorative machine stitchery. And yet the potential offered by automatic stitches has not been fully explored by most stitchers. As a friend said recently, "There has to be more to it than little duckies on children's clothes."

Yes, there is definitely more, especially when you begin to combine automatic stitches.

But first, here are some general guidelines to keep in mind as you explore automatic stitches:

■ If ever you needed a doodle cloth, this is the time. I have seen a tunic top with the front panel worked in solid decorative stitches—but the panel was badly rippled, destroying the beauty of the stitches, probably because the seamstress had not loosened the tensions. Try out each stitch you plan to use on a doodle cloth of exactly the same material as your article.

■ Strengthen your fabric. When I am working a long row of stitches, I almost always back my material with adding machine tape or typing paper, gently tearing it off later.

■ Be sure to watch the formation of the stitch in the slot of the presser foot, instead of watching the stitching line in front of the foot. This is particularly important when you are following a curving line.

■ Whenever possible, work the automatic stitches before cutting out pattern pieces.

■ Use the embroidery foot, since the grooves on the underside pass easily over previous rows of stitching.

The most obvious use of your decorative stitches is in the replacement of topstitching. Again, if you are planning extensive machine stitchery on clothing, do the work first before cutting out the garment. Cut off the excess tissue paper around your pattern piece and pin or weight it on the fabric. As a guideline, draw or machine baste around the edge of the pattern directly onto the fabric and then remove the pattern piece. I also machine baste along the seam line as an added guideline, since automatic stitches used as topstitching are generally spaced one presser foot width away from the *seam* line—not the line you have drawn to indicate the edge of the fabric.

The choice of thread for decorative topstitching is dependent on your background fabric. As a loose rule, I like to match the type of thread to the type of fabric—cotton thread with cotton fabric, wool thread with wool fabric, etc. Occasionally, when working decorative stitches with cotton thread, you will need a heavier line to make the pattern show up better, so use two threads. Either use two spools of the same thread or wind a bobbin full of cotton thread and put it on the second spool holder (if your machine doesn't have two, use the bobbin winding shaft). Thread both the regular spool thread and the second thread separately through all the thread guides and tension springs, as usual. If your needle shaft has guides for two threads, put one on each side; otherwise, thread the two threads together. You may need the help of a needle threader to coax both threads through the needle. Insert the needle threader from the back of the hole to the front, slide the threads through the gap in the needle threader wire, and pull the threader to the back again, which pulls the two threads through the needle easily (Diagram 43). Now do your automatic stitches on a doodle cloth, loosening tensions if necessary, and

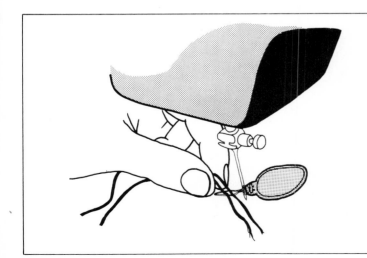

Insert the wire of the needle threader from the back to the front of the needle eye, thread the two ends through the gap in the wire, and pull the threader back through the eye.

Diagram 43

you will find that the double thread works beautifully. You can even use two colors of thread and achieve an unusual color mix. I have used blue and yellow thread together; this looks green from a distance and like a blue-yellow tweed up close.

As we discussed in Chapter 6, any thick thread can be wound into the bobbin and laid on the surface of your garment by working with the underside up. This is true for the automatic stitches too. Exquisite results can be had, for example, by winding metal threads, darning wool, or soft one-ply yarns (the kind used to knit baby sweaters) onto the bobbin, to become decorative stitches on the topside by working with the underside up. Use ordinary cotton sewing machine thread on top and adjust tensions, loosening bobbin and tightening top tensions, so that the thick thread lies on the surface of the fabric. (Plate 23)

Even with this method of working the underside up, I still use a piece of adding machine or typing paper, cello-taping the paper onto the underside of the fabric to hold the paper on securely, and drawing the line of stitching directly on the paper. Afterward, the paper is gently pulled off, using tweezers to remove any stubborn pieces.

Don't forget that many kinds of ribbon, cord, or braid can be attached to a background with automatic stitches. I like to work the ribbon separately. Stitch down the center of the ribbon and then apply it to the background by stitching the edges with more colorful rows of decorative stitches. (Plate 24)

When you are working a line of decorative stitches around a rectangle, such as a pocket, your motifs should match perfectly at the corner. To accomplish this, you must make two preparations: first, stitch six repeat motifs on a doodle cloth. As you sew, count exactly how many stitches form each pattern, so that you can stop the machine at the exact finish of the sixth pattern. Second, lay the doodle cloth on the stitching line of the article, with the finish of the sixth pattern exactly at the corner. Mark with pins backwards from the corner where each pattern must fall, using the doodle cloth as a guide. (Diagram 44)

Begin stitching a motif on the article exactly at the beginning of your marks. As you stitch, watch the slot in the embroidery foot. If at the beginning of a motif the needle does not enter the fabric exactly where you've marked, push the fabric gently with your fingers. The result will be a slightly longer pattern, but the next

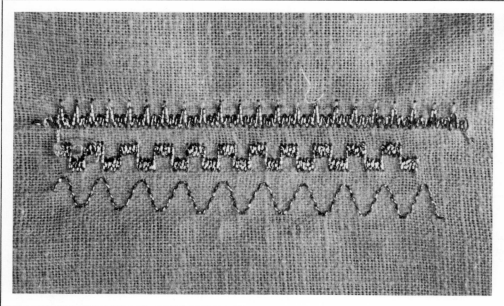

Plate 23
Metal threads can be wound onto the bobbin and used in decorative stitches worked from the underside of the fabric.

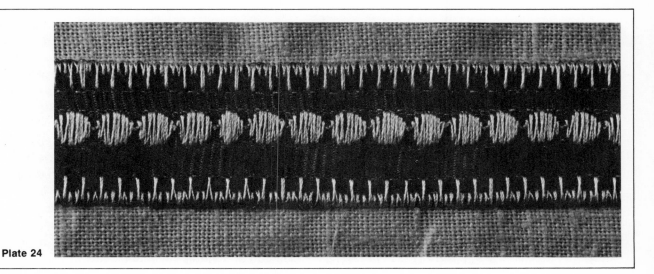

Plate 24

pattern will be perfect, and the corners will be perfect. Your fingers remain to the sides of each pattern, moving down to the next patterns, one by one. At the corner, sew the motif slowly so you have absolute control over the machine. You may want to hand turn the wheel for the last stitch of the motif. Leave the needle in the fabric after the last stitch, raise the presser bar lever, turn the fabric counterclockwise 90°, lower the presser bar lever, and begin the next line of stitching. Aren't you clever!

If your line of automatic stitching curves around a corner, don't try to change the direction of stitching in the middle of a motif. Imagine the curve to be made of small straight lines. Sew one motif on a straight line,

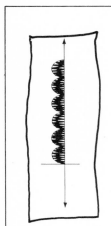

a Stitch six motifs on a doodle cloth, counting exactly how many stitches form one motif.

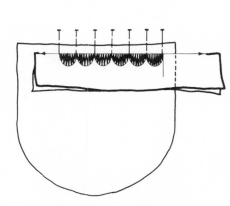

b Lay the doodle cloth on the stitching line of the pocket and mark backwards from the corner with pins. Mark all corners this way.

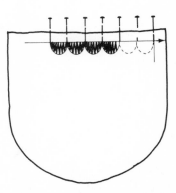

c Sew the decorative stitches, making sure each motif begins and ends at the pins. At the corner, leave the needle in the fabric and pivot the material. Continue stitching all the way around.

Diagram 44

Think of curved lines as a series of straight lines so that you will not curve in the middle of a motif, thereby ruining its formation.

Diagram 45

watching carefully through the slot of the presser foot. At the end of the motif, leave the needle in the fabric, raise the presser bar lever, move the fabric until you can see the line of stitching in the slot, lower the presser bar lever, and stitch another straight line of motif. Continue stitching one motif at a time. (Diagram 45)

Once you start experimenting with your automatic stitches, you quickly become hooked on their endless possibilities. Many of the stitches are not mirror images, as they are formed on either side of the needle. Therefore, by turning around 180° at the end of a line of decorative stitches and stitching a second row, you can create beautiful patterns. Look at the difference in effect of staggering one stitch in three ways. (Plate 25)

The patterns, of course, must fit together perfectly. A motif that is out of line or not symmetrical is disturbing to look at. Sew slowly and watch through the slot in the presser foot to be sure the beginning of a motif on the second line of stitching is perfectly matched to its counterpart on the first line of stitching. If it is not, push or hold back the fabric slightly with your fingers to elongate or shorten the pattern.

In addition to repeating one pattern, you can build new designs by combining rows of automatic stitches. Experiment on a doodle cloth to weed out the combinations that don't mix well.

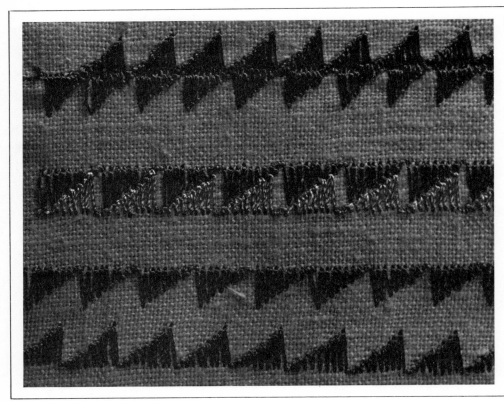

Plate 25

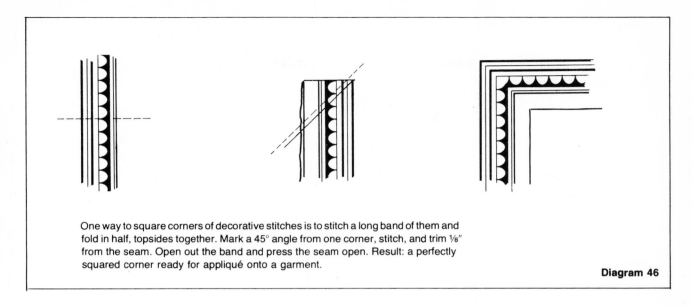

One way to square corners of decorative stitches is to stitch a long band of them and fold in half, topsides together. Mark a 45° angle from one corner, stitch, and trim ⅛″ from the seam. Open out the band and press the seam open. Result: a perfectly squared corner ready for appliqué onto a garment.

Diagram 46

Knowing how to handle squared corners for combination automatic stitches is important. There are three methods I like to use. First and easiest is to stitch the patterns on a separate band of material or a grosgrain ribbon. If the edges of the fabric are raw, turn them under ¼″(6mm). When you are done, fold the band, right sides together, and mark a 45° angle from one corner (I use a plastic right angle purchased at a stationery store). Straight stitch along the marked line, and cut ⅛″ (3mm) from this seam. Open out the band and press the seam open. Now appliqué the squared corner to the article, either with a straight stitch or with another decorative stitch. (Diagram 46)

The second method is to mark each corner with three parallel lines diagonal to the corner. I machine baste these guidelines so I can see them easily as I approach the corners. Work the automatic patterns from the two outside diagonal lines, stitching from the corners outward. Afterward, embroider one of the motifs on the remaining center diagonal line at the corner. (Plate 26)

The third method involves stitching around corners and takes more practice. Not all decorative stitches adapt easily to this, so try them on a doodle cloth first. Draw a diagonal line at each corner. On the line of stitching, mark six motifs away from the corner in each direction, as you did in Diagram 44 above. As you near a corner, make certain the motifs are falling in the correct places. Compensate if necessary by pushing or pulling the fabric slightly with your fingers. Leave the needle in the fabric at the corners, pivot counterclockwise 90°, and continue stitching. (Plate 27)

If you are stitching around a shape and two lines of stitching must meet exactly—that is, you must end the stitching exactly where you began—stop one stitch from the end. Carefully remove the fabric from the machine, pulling to the side away from the needle without jerking the fabric so that stitches are distorted. Pull one of the top threads to the back and tie off the ends. Then thread a tapestry needle with the remaining top thread and take the last stitch by hand, entering the fabric in the same hole where you started stitching. (Diagram 47)

Don't always think in terms of bands and borders of automatic stitches, because some of the patterns work well as isolated motifs. For example, to work a flower, baste or draw four intersecting lines as shown. On a doodle cloth sew several motifs to check the tensions and to count the exact number of stitches per motif. Stop the machine exactly after the last stitch of a motif has been sewn. On your article begin in the middle of the flower and sew one motif out, leaving the needle in

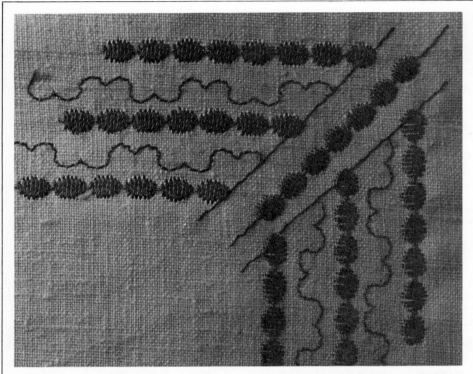

Plate 26
One way to square a corner with decorative stitches (but remove the basting stitches when done).

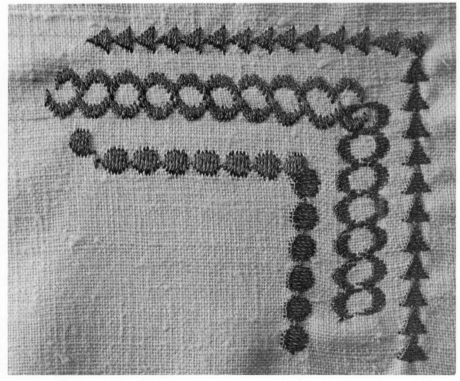

Plate 27
Not all decorative stitches go around corners gracefully. The inside stitch is not entirely successful, the middle stitch is acceptable, and the top stitch can only be worked by lifting the presser bar lever and moving the needle to a new starting point.

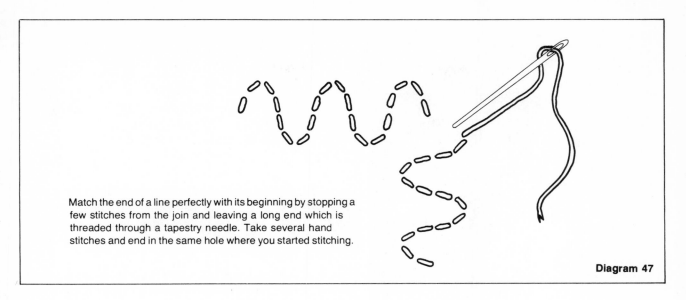

Match the end of a line perfectly with its beginning by stopping a few stitches from the join and leaving a long end which is threaded through a tapestry needle. Take several hand stitches and end in the same hole where you started stitching.

Diagram 47

the fabric at the end of the last stitch. Raise the presser bar lever and pivot the fabric 180°. Lower the presser bar lever and sew another motif, ending exactly in the middle and exactly at the end of the motif. If the needle on the last stitch is not entering the exact center, stop the machine and reposition the fabric so the needle will enter the exact center. If I am adamant about being exact it is because sloppiness results in distorted, unsettling flowers. Continue to sew from the middle out, along each of the eight lines radiating from the center.

After the last motif is sewn, raise the presser bar lever and gently pull the material to the side away from the needle. Turn the fabric over and tug on the bobbin thread until the loop of the top thread appears. Pull this loop through to the back and tie off the ends. (Diagram 48)

If your machine has a serpentine stitch, a very attractive chrysanthemum-like flower can be formed by stitching back and forth from a center point. Undoubtedly other decorative stitches based on an undulating

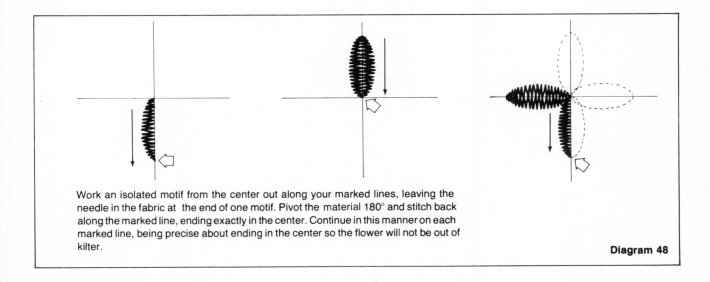

Work an isolated motif from the center out along your marked lines, leaving the needle in the fabric at the end of one motif. Pivot the material 180° and stitch back along the marked line, ending exactly in the center. Continue in this manner on each marked line, being precise about ending in the center so the flower will not be out of kilter.

Diagram 48

Plate 28

line of stitches can be similarly formed, so experiment on your own machine. (Plate 28)

Another spectacular use of serpentine stitch involves the use of a carpet fork (available in knitting and needlecraft stores—see Supply List—or made by bending a coat hanger into a U with square ends).

Wrap the fork with any thick thread—pearl cotton, 2- or 3-ply wool, variegated bouclé, etc. Then place a grosgrain ribbon under the fork and sew down the middle of the yarn, from the open end of the carpet fork to the closed end. Use the serpentine stitch if you have it; otherwise, a short straight stitch. Lock the last stitches by backstitching, remove everything from the machine, and pull out the carpet fork. You now have a colorful fringe to sew on a cape hood, purse strap, or baby bonnet. (Plate 29)

You also have the basis for a rug, believe it or not. You will need lots of yarn, backing canvas, or jute (available in rug-crafting and some needlework stores—see Supply List), and a carpet fork. Wind double strands of the yarn around the carpet hook, as explained above. On the canvas draw parallel lines 1″ (2,5cm) apart. Place the wound carpet hook on the canvas, with the left side of the fork on the middle line of the canvas. Stitch down the center of the hook with a short straight stitch or the serpentine stitch. When you reach the last of the yarn, leave the needle in the canvas and withdraw the fork carefully, until within an inch of its end. Rewind the carpet fork and sew as described above until you finish the row. For the next row, push the left edge of the wound fork firmly against the loops of the first row. After sewing this second row, cut the loops of the first row. Cut one row of loops each time you finish sewing a row. To keep the bulk minimal

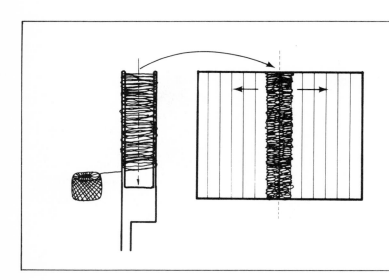

To make a carpet, mark the backing with parallel lines 1″ apart. Lay the wound fork along the center line and stitch down the center in a serpentine or straight stitch. Work from the center out, pushing each new row firmly against the previous row. Cut the loops for a rya-like rug.

Diagram 49

Plate 29   Wind a carpet fork or hairpin lace frame with heavy yarn. Stitch down the center and remove the frame for loops, fringe, or a carpet.

between the needle and the main body of the machine, work from the center of the rug to the right side. Turn the rug upside down 180° and again work from the center to the outside. Leave an inch all around the rug for a hem. Either turn it under and bind it by hand, or stitch carpet braid all around the outside. Paint the back with latex to keep the stitches from pulling out and the rug from slipping around the floor. (Diagram 49)

Each of the automatic stitches has its own potential, and as I said, not many people have yet probed the possibilities. For example, another special effect possible with automatic stitches simulates fagoting, which is a way to join two flat edges with embroidery. While experimenting, use two rectangles of fabric, both cut from a selvage. On a piece of typing paper draw three

parallel lines, each ⅛″ (3mm) apart. Lay one selvage on the left line and pin the fabric to the paper. Lay the other selvage along the right line and secure it to the paper. With the presser foot on and ordinary sewing machine thread in top and bobbin, set up the machine for overlock stitch (if you have it—otherwise a wide zigzag with a stitch length of 10-12 stitches/inch). (Plate 30)

Stitch down the paper so that the left side of the needle swing enters the middle pencilled line on the paper, and the right side enters the fabric. Turn the fabric around 180° and stitch down the remaining side as before, making sure that the needle pierces the paper exactly on top of the first row, and that on the other side of its swing, the needle pierces the fabric.

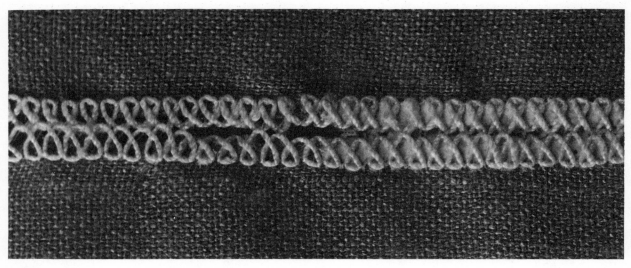

Plate 30
Machine faggoting has been worked with crochet cotton in the bobbin. The left third
is perfect, but if care is not taken to intersect the threads in the middle, gaps will
occur. At the right the paper has not been removed. If the paper is difficult to
extract, wet it and pull it out easily with tweezers.

o's . . .

- understand the guidelines at the beginning of this chapter
- whenever possible, do the embellishing before cutting out the garment
- experiment with automatic stitches, using heavy threads in the bobbin

AND DON'TS

- be sloppy about matching lines of automatic stitching
- watch the stitching line in front of the presser foot (instead of watching the stitch being formed)

Now carefully tear off the paper, using tweezers to remove any stubborn pieces, and separate the two rectangles of fabric. The result is very attractive fagoting. (Diagram 50)

Machine fagoting can be used on many garments and household articles, especially tablecloths, and is even more attractive if pearl or crochet cotton is wound into the bobbin and the fagoting is worked from the underside. You would still lay the paper with the lines on it *under* the fabric next to the needle case, even though you are working from the underside. Ordinary sewing machine thread in a matching color is used on top. The edges to be joined are overcast with a zigzag or seam binding and turned under before working the fagoting. Don't use a selvage as it would shrink more than the rest of the fabric. Wouldn't this be a charming way to lengthen a child's overalls or skirt?

Incidentally, that overlock stitch is quite becoming as topstitching when the stitch width is set at 0. Instead of stitching back and forth in a horizontal zigzag, it stitches back and forth in a straight line, giving you a heavier topstitching. This is particularly effective on leather and imitation suede fabrics.

I know two people who augment their income by skillful use of the automatic stitches. One is a dressmaker/artist who paints leather garments and

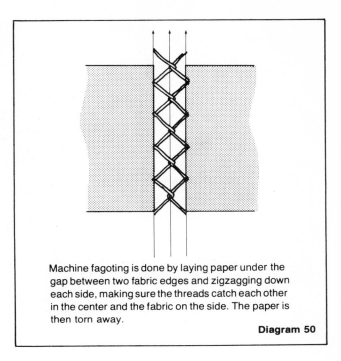

Machine fagoting is done by laying paper under the gap between two fabric edges and zigzagging down each side, making sure the threads catch each other in the center and the fabric on the side. The paper is then torn away.

Diagram 50

then emphasizes the design with automatic stitches. The other embellishes jeans and workshirts for a clothing store. There is definite money-making potential in these stitches, which may lessen the pain of the machine's price tag.

 Y HAT

(pictured in Color Plate 7)

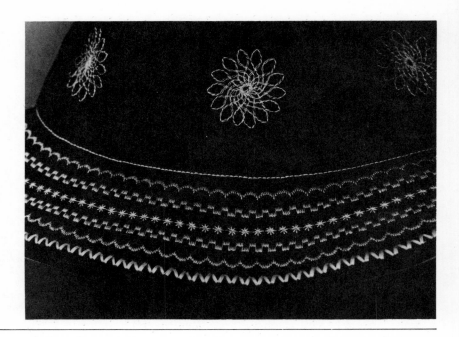

The brim of a hat is the ideal way to experiment with your machine's automatic stitches. Because each brand has slightly different patterns, you will have to substitute yours for mine; however I have tried to choose stitches basic to most machines and I've also given alternate ways of working the patterns.

you will need:

½ yd. (0,50m) firmly woven green cotton

½ yd. (0,50m) yellow lining, preferably the same kind of material as the green

fusible web interfacing

white extra-fine cotton, ordinary green and yellow sewing thread

any yarn to match the fabric (variegated, bouclé, etc.)

1 yd. (0,95m) of ¾″ (2cm) green grosgrain ribbon

hat pattern

doodle cloth of green and of green/yellow

pins, scissors, embroidery foot

one Velcro button (available in fabric stores)

step-by-step:

1 Pin the pattern pieces to the green cloth and cut out the hat. Only cut out one brim.

2 Cut out the lining, also with one brim.

3 Load the machine with a Size 10/11 (70) needle and the extra-fine white thread (also use it in the bobbin). Loosen top tension slightly and put on the embroidery foot. We will decorate the six hat sections first. The lovely chrysanthemum-like motif is done with the serpentine stitch and an automatic cam that makes the machine stitch back and forth from a central point. I stitched back and forth twice before pivoting the material, for a heavier line. You can also achieve this flower motif by starting at the central point and stitching one serpentine stitch motif. Stop the needle at the end of the motif and pivot the material 180°. Stitch back to the center and stop the needle in the fabric. Lift the presser bar lever and pivot the material not quite 180° and stitch as before, out and back. Continue all the way around the central point. You will definitely need to practice on a doodle cloth before attempting the real

SUMMARY OF TECHNIQUES

| | stitch | | tensions | | | |
	width	length	top	bobbin	foot	feed dog
automatic	varies	varies	varies	varies	embroidery	in place
fagoting	widest	10–12	loosen	normal	embroidery	in place

thing. (*Variation:* Load white pearl cotton on the bobbin, bypass bobbin tension, and work any isolated motif from the underside (see Diagram 48).

4 Sew the hat sections together, as explained in your pattern, and attach the lining. I changed to a Size 12 (80) needle and universal tension for this part.

5 Cut out a brim of fusible web interfacing. Pin it in place on the underside of the green brim. Right sides together, sew the two ends of the brim together at the seam line, catching in the interfacing. Press open carefully, taking care not to touch the iron to the visible fusible interfacing.

6 Sew the end seam of the yellow brim. Press open.

7 Lay the yellow brim on the green, matching right sides and seams. Sew the long bottom edge seam of the brim. Clip and turn rightside out. Press the two brims together, sealing them carefully with the fusible web interfacing.

8 Starting ¼″ (6mm) from the bottom of the brim, draw or baste 7 parallel lines each ¼″ (6mm) away from each other.

9 Set up a small doodle cloth that has exactly the same conditions as the brim—green fabric fused to yellow. Change back to a Size 10/11 (70) needle and white extra-fine thread top and bobbin. Test your tensions on the doodle cloth. I kept the bobbin at normal and loosened the top slightly.

10 To substitute your stitches for mine, study the photograph of the hat for the type of automatic stitch chosen. In the middle is a stitch that is a mirror image of itself on each side of the central line. To either side of that is a stitch that alternates from one side of the line to the other. The scallops must be worked so the curves face outward—check on your doodle cloth first. Start all stitches at the back seam and at the beginning of a motif.

11 Wind a carpet fork (or a hanger bent into a 1″[2,5cm]-wide U) with any yarn or floss you wish. It doesn't matter if it is washable or not. Why? You'll see in the following step #13.

12 Measure the brim of your hat with the grosgrain ribbon. Cut off enough for the ends to overlap 1″ (2,5cm) at the back seam. Satin stitch the ends of the grosgrain so they won't fray. (The rest of the ribbon is used inside the hat to bind the brim seam.)

13 Put green thread on top and set the machine for serpentine stitch or a close straight stitch. Lay the wound carpet fork on one end of the grosgrain ribbon and stitch down the middle. Leave 1″ (2,5cm) free at the end for the Velcro button. Sew on the button by hand or machine. (You can now take off the fringe when you want to wash the hat.)

14 Sew the brim to the hat as directed in your pattern.

15 Wasn't that one easy?!

ADDITIONAL IDEAS

■ Decorate a man's workshirt yoke using this chapter's automatic pattern sequence.

■ Join the shoulder seams of a wool cape with machine fagoting.

■ Make a rya-like rug in one day using a carpet fork.

■ Topstitch the seams of a bedspread with automatic stitches.

■ Stitch the letters of "June" of your fabric calendar by securing lime-green bias binding in the letter shapes to the backing with automatic stitches. (Half the year gone and you're still not paying attention? See Chapter 2—Additional Ideas.)

EIGHT

MACHINE ACCESSORIES

GLOSSARY

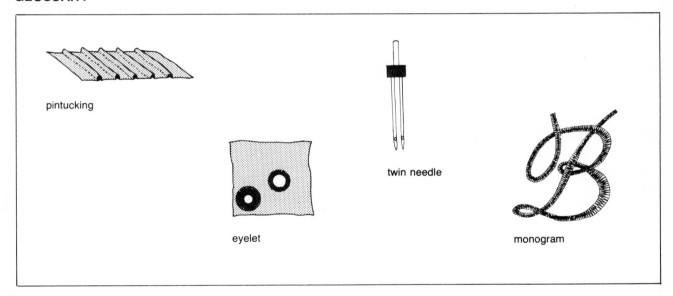

pintucking

eyelet

twin needle

monogram

THE TECHNIQUE

Once you are hooked on machine stitchery, you'll want to try some effects that require, or are made easier by, special equipment—presser feet, needles, and needle plates. Don't assume that the foot for a brand different from yours won't fit your machine. The feet are often interchangeable, depending on the length of the needle shaft and where the accessories attach (side, front, etc.). I take a presser foot from my machine with me when I shop; if it fits a different brand machine, the accessories for that machine will usually fit mine. Each brand has its own line of accessories. Check the competition when you're in the market for new equipment.

Plate 31 From the left: presser foot, embroidery foot, buttonhole foot, roller foot, pintucking foot, quilting guide, multiple cord foot.

There are many special presser feet for the sewing machine, with more coming out every day. I use the embroidery foot, with its grooves on the underside, whenever I do a lot of satin stitching or automatic stitches, because the foot moves easily over the previous buildup of threads. (Plate 31)

Two feet are useful for sewing on plastics (including vinyl), imitation leather, and leather: the roller foot and the Teflon embroidery foot. The roller foot prevents the friction which makes plastic stick to the sole of an ordinary presser foot. I also use the roller foot for sewing jersey-like knits.

The pintucking foot has spaced slots to help guide pintucks regularly through the foot. More about this below when we talk about twin needles.

I use the tailor tacking foot for more than marking darts and basting seams. Since it leaves behind a lovely loopy texture, I use it on items that won't be washed (pillows, wall hangings, etc.) as a suggestion of grass and seeds.

The hemmer foot speeds up this time-consuming process by folding under a seam allowance as you stitch. On thick corners I like to use the hemmer with my home-made felt wedge, which is made by folding a 3″ (7,5cm) felt square in half twice. With a straight stitch, sew along the two long parallel edges. When you approach the edge of, say, a tablecloth, where four thicknesses of cloth are waiting to harass your needle, place the short end of the felt wedge under the hemmer foot, against the edge of one hem. The foot rises over the graduated thickness of the felt without getting stuck on the added bulk of the tablecloth corners. At the corner, I sink the needle into the fabric, raise the presser bar lever, pivot the material counterclockwise 90°, place the felt wedge behind the presser foot against the edge of the tablecloth, lower the presser bar lever, and stitch the remaining hem. (Plate 32)

The quilting guide helps to quilt accurately in the middle of large pieces of fabric. Always start from the middle of the fabric and sew outwards. Be sure the quilting guide is not pressing hard on the material, but resting lightly on the surface; otherwise it will make the fabric slide around. I also use the quilting guide anytime I cannot see the guide marks on the needle plate—for example, I recently decorated the yoke of a ready-made workshirt with automatic stitches. I used the quilting guide to keep uniform the distance of the stitches from the edge of the yoke.

The multiple cord foot is fun to experiment with. I like to put four different colors of crochet cotton in the holes

Plate 32

and stitch over them with the serpentine stitch. A variation of this is to wind the elastic thread into the bobbin and then to stitch over the cords with the serpentine stitch. It makes a beautifully gathered edge on a sleeve.

The braiding foot is similar to the hemmer foot in guiding braid, soutache, or cord evenly through the foot. Automatic stitches worked on top of these trims is very attractive.

There are three special needles that give unusual effects to decorative machine stitchery: twin needles, the wing needle, and the wedge needle.

The variety of ways twin needles can be used is vast. The most straightforward use of them is decorative top stitching of seams. The twin-needle stitch is formed on the underside the same way a single stitch is formed, except that the bobbin hook grabs two loops of top thread instead of one. Therefore if you want your twin needle topstitching to lie flat, you must loosen upper tension. It would be nice to be able to lay two parallel thick threads on the surface in one operation (that is, with twin needles); however, unlike straight stitching with a heavier thread in the bobbin, you cannot stitch from the underside with twin needles and expect the heavier thread to be laid on the surface in

parallel lines of topstitching. (Diagram 51)

Pintucking, which is a second use of twin needles, is formed when you do not loosen upper tension. The tightness of your upper tension determines how much in relief your fabric is pulled. The use of the pintucking foot allows you to space rows of pintucking accurately.

Another way to increase the bumpiness of your pintucks is to back the fabric you are pintucking with

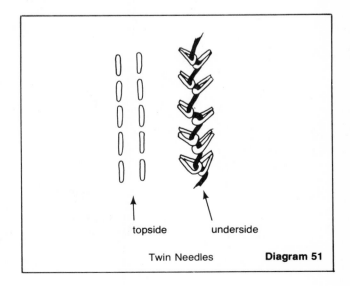

topside   underside

Twin Needles   **Diagram 51**

organza. Run your lines of pintucking. Then thread a tapestry needle with heavy yarn or thread—up to the size of rug yarn—and from the underside, run a line of this yarn into the channel formed by the twin needles between the organza and the fabric. If the garment is washable, don't use wool yarn. And if the pintucking is rounded or squared, leave a small loop outside the channel at these points, to allow for shrinkage when washing. (Diagram 52)

An alternate method for this extra-raised effect is to guide a heavy thread under the fabric as you stitch, which is then caught in the pintuck channel. (Diagram 53)

Turning squared corners with the twin needles must be done in three or four small stitches. Stop the machine with just the points of the needles in the fabric.

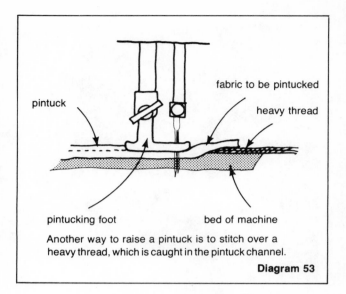

Another way to raise a pintuck is to stitch over a heavy thread, which is caught in the pintuck channel.

Diagram 53

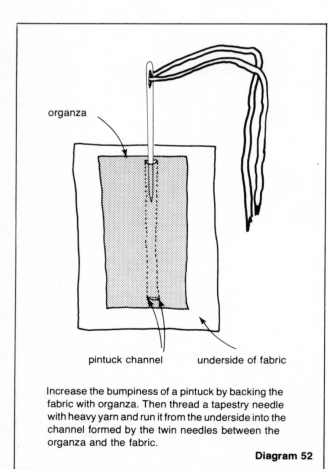

Increase the bumpiness of a pintuck by backing the fabric with organza. Then thread a tapestry needle with heavy yarn and run it from the underside into the channel formed by the twin needles between the organza and the fabric.

Diagram 52

Raise the presser bar lever and half-turn the fabric (less than 45°). Lower the presser bar lever and hand-turn the wheel to take one tiny stitch, leaving just the points of the needles in the fabric. Repeat these small turns until you are around the corner and then continue pintucking. (Diagram 54)

I like to use the twin needles to help me mark fabric for smocking. I run parallel lines of double stitching across a rectangle, the top and bottom of which I have marked with machine basting. I then hand-smock the fabric (Diagram 55). Remember to cut out the garment piece *after* smocking. Work the smocking or pintucking area and then lay the pattern piece on top of the fabric. If there is a skirt or full area under or above (as in a sleeve) the worked area do not stretch out the fabric for cutting, because when the garment is constructed, it will not hang right. Cut the sides of a dress, for example, on the straight of the fabric, with the fullness allowed to bunch under the pattern piece. (Diagram 56)

Twin needles combined with automatic stitches are quite beautiful. In particular, the serpentine stitch lends a captivating color and pattern to otherwise ordinary materials. The only thing you need to watch is that the width of your stitch is not so wide that the twin needles hit the presser foot or needle plate. This would also happen if you left the needle decentered from a previous project.

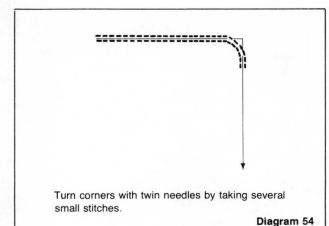

Turn corners with twin needles by taking several small stitches.

Diagram 54

automatic stitches that stitch into a central hole several times for a very attractive look.

If a line of zigzag worked with the wing needle is sewn ¼″ (6mm) away from the bottom of a piece of organza, and then the fabric is trimmed along one side of the zigzag, a lovely picot effect is made. More on the visual effects of the wing needle in Chapter 9. (Plate 33)

There are many special needle plates available to the adventuresome machine stitcher. One of my favorites is the eyelet plate. This usually comes with an awl for piercing the fabric, to make a hole big enough to fit over the eyelet shaft on the plate. Work eyelets with the fabric on a hoop, stretching the material before making

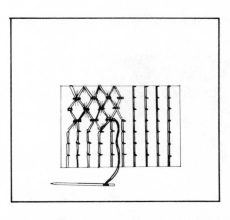

Use the twin needles to mark a fabric for smocking. If you have a blind hem stitch, set it for a narrow jag (otherwise the twin needles will hit the needle plate) and line up each row accurately. Smock from mark to mark.

Diagram 55

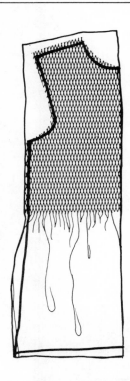

Smock a material before cutting out the garment piece. Then allow the material to bunch under the smocking and lay the pattern over it for cutting. Do not pull out the material flat under the smocking because the garment will not lay flat.

Diagram 56

Don't forget that you can free machine embroider with twin needles, which can give a delicate shadow effect.

A second unusual needle is the wing needle (also called a hemstitch needle) which makes large holes and is especially lovely on fine fabrics like organza. The wing needle can be used in combination with the

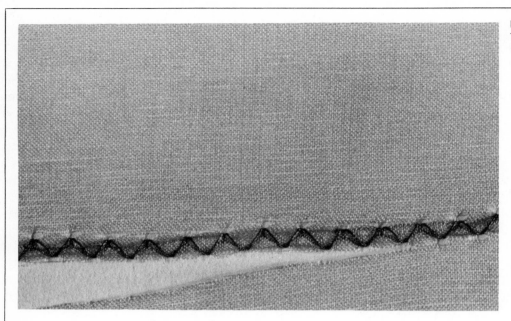

Plate 33
The picot edge is made with the wing needle and an open zigzag.

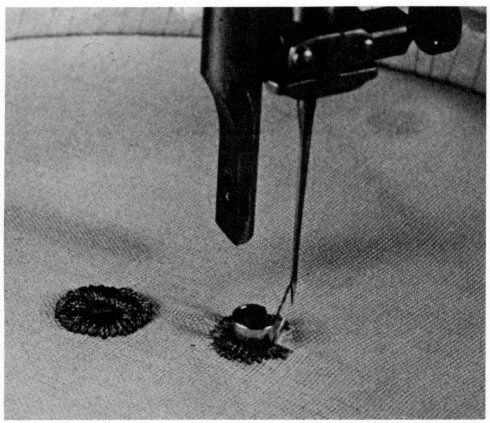

Plate 34
On the left is an eyelet made over felt. On the right is an eyelet in progress.

the hole with the awl. You will have to remove both the foot and the needle to fit the hoop into the eyelet plate and will not be able to use any foot (unless your machine has a special eyelet foot). Decenter the needle to the left and don't forget to lower the presser bar lever. It is important to run both the machine and the hoop at a constant, medium speed so that the eyelets will be evenly formed. Stitch around at least three times for each eyelet. To end off, decenter the needle to the right, change the stitch width to 0, and take several stitches in one place to lock the threads. (Plate 34)

I have tried several methods to pad eyelets. One is to use crochet cotton in the bobbin and work with the underside of the fabric up, in order to make a heavier line of satin stitch. Decrease bobbin tension and tighten upper tension. Another is to make a small felt cutout, to be stitched over. Poke the awl through the felt first and then cut out a circle 1/8″ (3mm) around the hole. Coax this felt doughnut over the eyelet shaft and loosen top and bobbin tensions. As you sew, hold the felt down on the side opposite where the stitches are being formed. A third way to pad an eyelet is to use a bead that has a big enough hole and is low enough for the zigzag needle to clear. Stitch over the bead for a nice raised effect. Always experiment first on a doodle cloth.

Some machines have extended needle plates to sew circular designs. The fabric must be stiffened with a backing, though, as it is apt to pull out of shape when stitching in circles. These plates are not cheap. There is a less expensive (but not as accurate) way to stitch circular designs. Decide how large you want your circle and measure the distance from the center of the circle to one side (the radius). To the left of the hole in the needle plate, cello-tape a thumbtack upside down, a radius away from the hole. Back your fabric with organza, or whatever you prefer, and put it into a hoop. Stick the fabric over the thumbtack whenever you want the center of the circle to fall on the fabric. Now, to hold everything together, put an eraser onto the point of the thumbtack sticking through the fabric. Without stretching the fabric out of shape, keep the fabric taut between the thumbtack and the needle, as you sew slowly and carefully in a perfect circle. (Diagram 57)

Another device that some machines have is a template for perfect monogramming. It is similar to the quilting guide in that you watch an extension to the

Do's . . .

- look at the accessories made for other brand machines with the same needle shaft length and clamping device as yours
- make yourself a felt wedge for thick corners
- experiment
- keep up-to-date on new accessories by talking to your sewing machine dealer

AND DON'TS

- decenter the needle when you are using twin needles

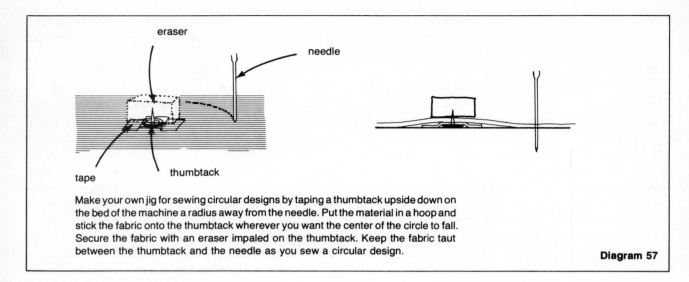

eraser

needle

tape

thumbtack

Make your own jig for sewing circular designs by taping a thumbtack upside down on the bed of the machine a radius away from the needle. Put the material in a hoop and stick the fabric onto the thumbtack wherever you want the center of the circle to fall. Secure the fabric with an eraser impaled on the thumbtack. Keep the fabric taut between the thumbtack and the needle as you sew a circular design.

Diagram 57

right of the machine, and by making it follow a stencil cutout of a letter, you make a perfect satin-stitched monogram. For directions on a more free-hand monogram, see Chapter 10.

Be sure to ask your sewing machine dealer what new special equipment has been developed for the various machines, so you can constantly expand your repertoire of decorative machine stitchery.

$\mathcal{A}$MERICANA HANDBAG

(pictured in Color Plate 5)

This design takes advantage of the elegant simplicity of imitation leather and uses the following machine accessories: roller foot, quilting guide and twin needles. It also calls on your aptitude for couching-by-piercing, machine quilting, heavy thread in the bobbin, and several-layered appliqué.

---

you will need:

1 yd. (0,95m) 36″ (90cm) imitation leather

1 yd. (0,95m) 36″ (90cm) lining fabric

1 chamois cloth (used for washing cars) purchased at a supermarket or hardware store

small amount of Dacron batting

white organza

white and gold crochet cotton

brown extra-fine rayon, nylon invisible, white, and black cotton threads

roller foot, quilting guide, twin needles, darning foot

small doodle cloth of imitation leather

scissors, pins, tissue paper, felt-tip pen, pencil, hoop

step-by-step:

1 Enlarge the handbag and eagle cartoon (Diagram 58) so that the finished size with seam allowances is about 19¼″ (49,2cm) x 15¼″ (38,6cm).

2 Fold the imitation leather in half, pin the pattern in place, and cut out the handbag, *adding* ½″ (1,3cm) seams on all edges. (If you cut out the two handbag pieces separately, be sure to turn the pattern face-down before cutting the second piece.) Cut out the lining in the same manner.

3 Place the tissue paper over the blown-up cartoon and trace the eagle with the felt-tip pen. Cut away excess tissue paper.

4 Pin the eagle to the imitation leather and cut the entire wing span in one piece, ignoring the eagle's head and haunch area by cutting straight across behind the tissue paper to connect the two wings.

5 Cut out each of the four upper wing areas separately from imitation leather. Also cut out the two haunches and the main body (in all, seven pieces).

6 Put the Dacron batting on the organza and lay the wing span on top. Pin it securely in place.

7 Load the machine with brown extra-fine rayon thread on top and anything on the bottom. Put on the

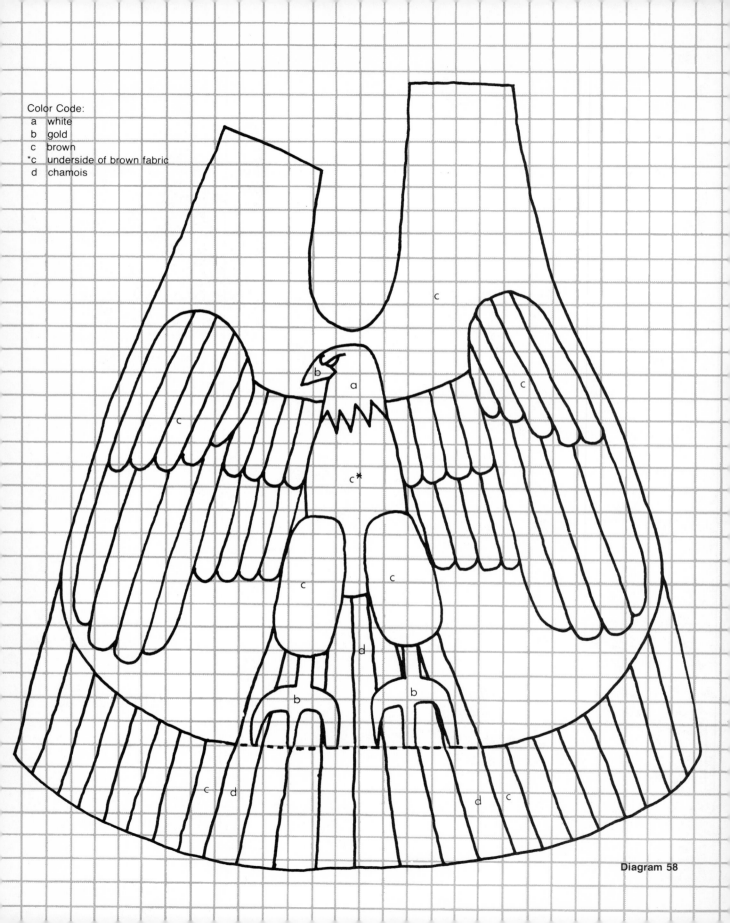

Color Code:
a   white
b   gold
c   brown
*c underside of brown fabric
d   chamois

Diagram 58

roller foot and decrease presser foot tension (if possible on your machine). Loosen top tension slightly.

8 Using 10-12 stitches/inch, sew ¼" (6mm) in from the edge all around the eagle, using lots of finger control to keep the fabric from moving. Don't try to swing around each individual feather tip; just curve smoothly around the bottom edge.

9 Put the quilting guide next to the roller foot on the machine. Start at the bottom edge of the right wing and sew a straight line in the crevice between feathers (see cartoon) three-quarters of the way up the wing. The remainder will be covered by the upper wing.

10 Set the needle in the second crevice and quilting guide in the first. Sew another straight line. Continue sewing until the bottom wings are quilted.

11 If the chamois cloth from the supermarket is wrinkled, press it from the underside with a warm steam iron. Lay the tail and feet part of your cut-up tracing on the chamois and trace around the tail with a soft pencil. The bottom part of the tail below the feet will become part of the fringe.

12 Load the machine with two spools of white cotton thread on top, the twin needles, and white thread below. Practice pintucking on a part of the chamois you won't need. I tightened both upper and lower tensions considerably.

13 Pintuck three rows on the tail, as shown on the cartoon.

14 Cut the feet from the tracing, position on the chamois, and trace around with the pencil.

15 Load invisible thread in the top, Size 12 (80) needle, return bobbin tension to normal, and loosen top tension. Put on the darning foot. Lay gold crochet cotton along the outline of the feet and secure it to the chamois by couching-by-piercing or a narrow zigzag. Fill in the feet completely. (It takes longer to use crochet cotton than a fuzzy yarn but I like the sheen.) Change the top thread to brown rayon and outline the

feet in a free-machined straight stitch. Press from the underside.

16 Now begins the assembly of the eagle. It isn't difficult but it takes forever to describe. Lay the four upper wings in position. The machine is already loaded with brown rayon and the tensions correct. After putting on the roller foot, stitch from the bottom of the upper wings to the top, quilting the crevices as you did in Step 9.

17 Turn the quilted wings over and trim away the excess organza and batting close to the outline stitching.

18 Pin or tape the wing span into place on one side of the handbag and carefully stitch ⅛" (3mm) from the edge, taking care not to let the fabric shift or pucker. (The truth is, I hand-basted here.)

19 Cut out the chamois tail and pin it in position on the handbag below the wings and main body. Stitch from the seam line of the handbag up one side, across the top, and down the other side of the tail to the seam line.

20 Turn the main body piece of the eagle over so the underside is up and pin into position in between the wings. Stitch all around. Yes, *underside*—it gives a subtle texture variation.

21 Pin the two haunches into place over the main body and stitch all around.

22 Lay the white organza over the eagle's head and trace with a pencil. Put the organza into a hoop, underside up.

23 Load the machine with white ordinary cotton on top and white crochet cotton in the bobbin (see Chapter 6 for winding heavy threads onto a bobbin). Loosen bobbin tension to 0 and tighten top tension. Put on the darning foot.

24 Stitch the white part of the head by filling top to bottom in rows of free-machined straight stitch close together.

SUMMARY OF TECHNIQUES

	stitch		tensions				
	width	length	top	bobbin	foot	feed dog	comments
pintucking	0	10-12	tighten	normal	pintuck	in place	
picot	1–4	10–12	universal		presser	in place	use wing needle
eyelet	1–4	0	universal		none	eyelet plate	use hoop
monogram	1–4	0	loosen	normal	darning	lower	use hoop and extra-fine thread

25 Turn the organza over in the hoop so the topside is up. Put ordinary white thread in the bobbin and invisible nylon on top. Loosen top tension and return bobbin to normal. Fill in the beak area with the gold crochet cotton the same way you did the feet.

26 Load black in the top and free-machine satin stitch the eye.

27 Take the organza out of the hoop and cut close to the eagle's head. If its height seems too low in comparison to the rest of the body, tuck some Dacron batting behind it before stitching it in place with a black satin stitch.

28 Cut out the three pieces of imitation leather fringe and pin two each to each side of the bottoms of the handbag, matching right sides to right sides. The fringe does not hang loose yet. It is nestled against the main parts of the handbag along with the tail of the eagle which should be turned up against the eagle so as not to be caught in the seams.

29 Put the right sides of the bags together and sew the 1-2 and 3-4 ½″ (1,3cm) seams. Press open.

30 Sew the outside edge in a ½″ (1,3cm) seam from 5 to 6 and clip the curves. Turn the bag right side out.

31 Cut out two handbag pieces of lining fabric *adding* ½″ (1,3cm) seams all around. Follow Steps 29 and 30 for assembling the lining but don't turn it right side out.

32 Shove the bag inside the lining so right sides are touching. Match the top two seams. Sew a ½″ (1,3cm) seam along the inner opening (2-3-2). Clip curves.

33 To turn the bag right side out, pull the imitation leather through one of the openings and push the lining inside the bag.

34 Slip stitch the remaining edges closed and topstitch with the roller foot and the brown extra-fine rayon.

ADDITIONAL IDEAS

■ Appliqué the eagle of this chapter's project to the backs of dining room chairs.

■ Pintuck the yoke and lower two-thirds of a short-sleeved dress before cutting out the garment.

■ Make picots on the lower edge of ruffled curtains.

■ Work a neck-piece shape flat with solid eyelets. Then cut it out and sew the neck edge over flexible wire, to be shaped to fit your neck.

■ Use the twin needles to mark a long red rectangle for white hand-smocking. When finished, seam this panel to another blue rectangle of fabric on which you have monogrammed a white "July" for your fabric calendar. (Been on vacation? See Chapter 2— Additional Ideas.)

NINE

𝒯RANSPARENT FABRICS

GLOSSARY

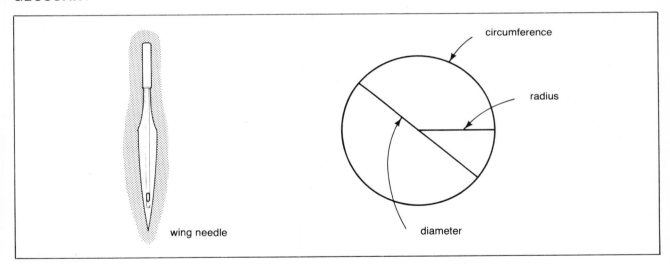

wing needle

circumference

radius

diameter

THE TECHNIQUE

The transparent fabrics like net and organza are usually linked with bedroom curtains and wedding veils. Yet when worked with machine embroidery, the see-through quality of any transparent fabric, combined with the shadow of the bobbin thread, creates an unusual dimension.

What are some of the transparent fabrics? Organza, organdy, net, scrim, gauze, chiffon, some muslins. Since these fabrics are not familiar to many, ask your fabric store to show you the variety of weights and textures available.

It is also quite useful to have on your bookshelf a guide to fiber and fabric terms. For example, I often advise you to back a fabric with organza or organdy.

But what is the difference between them? From my BUTTERICK FABRIC HANDBOOK, "At one time, organdy was a sheer, lightweight, open cotton fabric with a stiff finish; organza was the same fabric made of silk. Today, those former distinctions have almost disappeared and the names organdy and organza are used almost as synonyms. The natural fibers have been replaced by man-made fibers for their manufacture. Permanent finishes on natural fiber organdy and man-made fiber organdy have eliminated the largest objection to this fabric—its tendency to wrinkle easily and its loss of crispness. Organdy is always popular for curtains and is often used in clothing, especially for blouses and evening wear."

Other uses for machine embroidered transparent fabrics besides blouses and evening wear are lampshades, wall hangings, room dividers, and window pictures reminiscent of stained glass.

This last effect, a form of reverse appliqué, is done by stacking up layers of colored organza (or any transparent fabric you like). With a Size 10 (70) needle and extra-fine thread, sew lines of satin stitch in an interesting pattern and then cut down through the layers, close to the satin stitch, to whatever color you want to show through. Even four or five layers of the same color can be worked this way, the effect of three layers of the same color being a deeper tone than one layer. Of course this same reverse appliqué technique can be worked on any fabric. Likewise, any of the techniques discussed earlier in the book adapt beautifully to the transparent fabrics. (Plate 35)

Zigzag or automatic stitches, worked with extra-fine thread and a wing needle (see Chapter 8) on transparent fabrics, are quite fetching. The large wing needle makes big holes in the fabric and the overall effect has a lacey, trellis-like look. Starting at the right side, stitch a line of wide zigzag with a stitch length of 10-12 stitches per inch. At the end of the row, leave the needle in the left side of the work and pivot the material 180°. Sew another row of zigzag, making sure that on the left side the wing needle enters the same hole as the first row. Continue these rows until you have a piece of hemstitching wide enough for your purpose (Diagram 59). It is possible to fill small areas with hem-

Plate 35
Layers of silk organza are stacked up and put into a hoop. A design is worked with narrow zigzag and some layers are cut away for reverse appliqué.

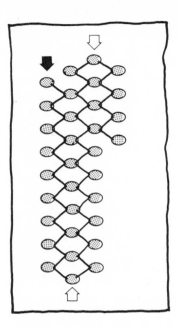

Hemstitching can be started from either the right or left side. From the left, begin hemstitching with the wing needle at the black arrow using a wide open zigzag. At the bottom of the row leave the needle in the fabric on the right side of the zigzag and pivot the material 180°. Stitch the second row so that on the right side the needle enters the same hole as the first row. Continue in this manner.

Diagram 59

through area falls at a crucial point, back the lace with a different color fabric—the effect is riveting).

Manipulation of machine tensions, used in conjunction with the transparent fabrics, adds an extra dimension to your work. When either top or bobbin tension is loosened, the loops of thread either throw a shadow on the surface of the fabric or create a shadow under it. One of my favorite fabrics to work on for free machine embroidery is organza, because while it is lightweight, it is woven stiffly enough to be able to maneuver freely without a hoop. For sure, don't back organza with paper because when you tear away the paper, the threads pull the organza out of shape.

Once again, let me harp about the importance of a doodle cloth for experimenting. The time to discover whether or not a technique looks good or puckers badly is *before* you tackle the actual project.

One of the most exciting techniques I've learned is similar to cut work in hand embroidery. It works up beautifully on transparent fabrics, but can also be

stitching directly on the backing fabric, but another way to insert hemstitching is to lay the trellised rectangle onto a transparent backing and satin stitch any shape. Cut the hemstitching close to the outside of the satin stitch without cutting the backing fabric. Then turn the work over and cut away the backing fabric within the satin stitch shape. (Plate 36)

This same insertion technique can be used with ready-made lace. Lay either a strip of lace or one motif from a lace panel on top of the fabric and satin stitch down or around the edge. Then carefully cut away the background fabric from the underside. This technique is attractively used to insert lace on the sleeves of a blouse, either crosswise or lengthwise, and as isolated motifs inserted anywhere on garments (if the see-

Plate 36 To hemstitch small shapes, work the hemstitching separately and apply to another fabric. Then cut away the fabric in back of the hemstitching.

adapted for any closely woven fabric. Stretch your fabric in a hoop and set up the machine for free machine embroidery: Size 10/11 (70) needle, stitch length 0, universal tension, darning foot on, and feed dogs covered or lowered (both optional—I use the darning foot and don't bother with the feed dogs). For your first attempt, trace around a quarter so your cut work will really look like a circle instead of an amoeba. Put the hoop and fabric under the needle, bring up the bobbin thread, and lock the first stitch. Stitch a straight stitch in free machine embroidery about three times around the pencilled circle. This is to strengthen the fabric, because the next thing you do is to remove the hoop from under the needle and cut away the circle close to the stitching (but don't remove the fabric from the hoop). Now put the fabric back under the needle, bring up the bobbin thread anywhere on the circumference of the circle, and lock the first stitch. Since your stitches could pull loose if you didn't take care, stitch one-quarter of the way around the circle, right on top of your previous stitching, and stop with the needle in the fabric. Now drive the machine at a fast speed while you stitch *across* the circle. You'd think the machine would

object to stitching on thin air, but if you make it go fast enough, the threads merely twist around each other. When you reach the opposite side of the circle, take a few stitches in the same place to lock the threads to the fabric and then stitch along the circumference half-way around the circle. Now stitch across the circle to the far side again, making an X in the center. Take a few stitches in the same place to lock the threads and stitch a short way along the circumference to bisect one of the four pie shapes. Stitch across the circle, running the machine fast, lock the threads on the opposite side, and stitch along the circumference to the middle of another pie shape. This time run the twisted threads to the center intersection only. Then stitch in spirals from the center out, as if you were making a spider web. Quit spiralling whenever you're pleased, and stitch out to the edge in the middle of the remaining pie shape. Lock stitches at the edge, as before. If you wish, satin stitch the edge of the circle and embellish this edge with free machine straight stitch. (Plate 37)

As I said, this method works well in other fabrics and the cut-out part does not have to be worked in a circular design. Study hand cut work for ideas. The twists of

Plate 37
On the left is a circle worked in cutwork. On the right is a cutwork circle in progress. The needle is just about to stitch to the center for spiralling.

thread can also be thickened by satin stitch worked over them.

In a similar vein, the threads on loosely woven transparent fabrics like scrim and curtain netting can be satin stitched both vertically and horizontally to give the impression of needleweaving. (Plate 38)

One of the handcrafts that can be easily adapted to the machine is the making of stocking-face dolls. I like to use the glazed-back Dacron batting for filler, but loose batting can be used if it is backed with a piece of organza. Cut a 4″ (10cm) tall tube from pantyhose or nylons. Cut and open out the tube to lie flat, place it over the batting, and back it with organza if you want. Using a Size10/11 (70) needle and extra-fine cotton or rayon sewing machine thread, free machine embroider a face on the nylon. If you wish, you may sculpt the face first by pinching a nose and cheeks. Try to plan your direction of stitching so that the entire face can be stitched in one operation. I usually start at the side of any eyebrow next to a temple (Diagram 60). When you have completed the face, cut off the extra organza on the back and put another wad of batting behind the face. Draw the nylon around the wad to the

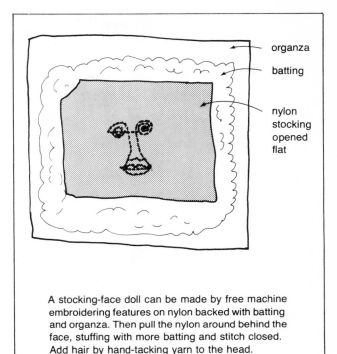

organza

batting

nylon stocking opened flat

A stocking-face doll can be made by free machine embroidering features on nylon backed with batting and organza. Then pull the nylon around behind the face, stuffing with more batting and stitch closed. Add hair by hand-tacking yarn to the head.

Diagram 60

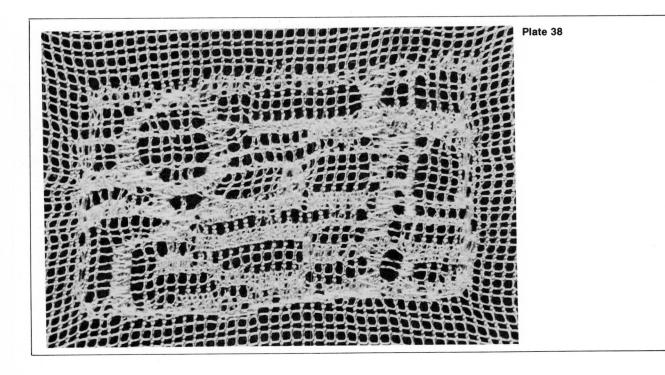

Plate 38

Plate 39
Prairie Schoolmarm

DO'S . . .

- ■ work hemstitching first and then appliqué it to garments
- ■ experiment on a doodle cloth first
- ■ try everything you've learned about machine stitchery on the transparent fabrics

AND DON'TS

- ■ leave your Size 10/11 (70) needle on the machine when you finish a project back and stitch it all together. Then work the stuffing inside the head back and forth with your fingers until you are pleased with the modeling of the face. Add hair by hand-stitching yarn over the head. (Plate 39)

In closing, I hope I've inspired you to experiment on all the transparent fabrics with the techniques you've learned so far—net and printed voile, for example, both work magnificently. And don't forget the subtle tones you can achieve by layering transparent fabrics over solid fabrics.

Do remember, though, to take the Size 10/11 (70) needle off the machine when you finish working with the transparent fabrics and replace it with the normal Size 12/14 (80/90) needle.

⊙ELIGHTFUL LAMPSHADE

Nothing is quite as entrancing as light shining through layers of transparent fabric. Hence, this chapter's design is decoration for a purchased lampshade, using lace, silk organza, and hemstitching with a wing needle. (See the Supply List for a mail order source of lampshades in many sizes and shapes.)

you will need:

1 yd. (0,95m) purple silk organza
fusible web interfacing
purchased lampshade
purple extra-fine cotton sewing thread

elastic thread
tissue paper, pins, scissors, tape, pencil
lace (and purple dye, if necessary)

step-by-step:

1 Since each lampshade is a different shape, here's how to make a pattern for yours. Wrap a wide strip of tissue paper around your lampshade and tape the paper securely over the bottom edge. Now fold and pleat the tissue paper until it conforms to the shape of your lampshade. Tape it over the top edge and tape all the pleats down. Run a pencil along the top and bottom edges. Now gently remove all the tape from the top and bottom edges and lay the pattern out flat. If your lampshade is shaped like mine, the pattern should be a curving arc. Add 1" (2,5cm) at the top and bottom edges for turn-over and ½" (1,3cm) at each side of the back seam.

2 Divide the arc into sections, depending on how large your lampshade is. I've used roughly 7" (18cm) areas for the hearts (Diagram 61) and 2" (5cm) for the

hemstitching and lace. Before making the actual lampshade, first draw the divisions and designs on your pattern paper with pencil, in case you need to change the proportions for your lampshade.

3 Cut two or three lampshade covers from your pattern (number of layers depends on how sheer and light-colored your organza is).

4 Load the machine with the wing needle and the purple extra-fine thread, top and bottom. Set the machine for an open zigzag (widest stitch width, 10-12 stitches/inch). Experiment on a doodle cloth to find the perfect tension.

5 Cut a rectangle of purple organza 2" (5cm) wide and four times the width of your lampshade (mine is 6½"

Diagram 61

(16,3cm) + 1″ (2,5cm) at the top and at the bottom). Starting at the right side of the rectangle, stitch a line of open zigzag. At the bottom, stop the needle in the fabric on the left side and pivot the material 180°. Stitch another row of open zigzag, making sure that on the left side the wing needle enters the holes of the previous row of zigzag. Continue until the entire rectangle is hemstitched.

6 Change the wing needle to a Size 10/11 (70) needle and zigzag the edges of the rectangle. Lay the hemstitched rectangle on the top layer of organza as marked on your pattern and zigzag the rectangle to the organza. Cut off the part of the rectangle you will use for the other hemstitched parts. Lay the lace on top of the edges of the hemstitched rectangle and zigzag them into place. (I had to dye my lace purple—easy.) Turn the organza over and carefully cut away the part under the lace and hemstitched rectangle. Repeat for all the hemstitched areas.

7 Cut two rectangles of purple organza, 7″ (18cm) by 9″ (23cm). Cut a piece of fusible web interfacing to fit between the two layers. Fuse the organza together with a warm iron.

8 Trace one heart from the cartoon and use it as a template to cut out 21 hearts from the fused rectangle.

9 Cut three pieces of fusible web interfacing the size of the entire heart area (see Step 2). Put the web over the cartoon and trace the heart arrangement with pencil. Lay the bottom piece of organza down, put the fusible web interfacing in place, lay the seven hearts per motif in place, cover with the second (top) layer of organza, and fuse all together. Repeat three times. If you have trouble with your hearts moving around, touch the *tip* of a warm iron to the center of a heart to secure it. Be careful not to touch any of the exposed fusible web with the iron.

10 Zigzag the upper edge of the organza to keep it from fraying and turn it under ½″ (1,3cm). Press. Cut a piece of elastic thread the circumference of the shade at the top. On the underside of the turned edge, lay the elastic thread ¼″ (6mm) from the top edge and zigzag over it, pulling the thread *slightly*. This will gather the top edge securely.

11 Sew the ½″ (1,3cm) back seam. Press open. Finish edges if desired.

12 Slip the lampshade over the lamp and mark the bottom edge with a white pencil. (If the organza pulls upward too much, you have pulled the elastic too tight as you sewed. In this case, zigzag the bottom edge as you did in Step 10 and stitch elastic on the underside of the bottom.) Otherwise, you can use the wing needle and a wide open zigzag to picot the bottom edge (see Plate 33, page 104), making sure the wing needle enters the white line you penciled on the right side of its swing.

SUMMARY OF TECHNIQUES

	stitch		tensions				
	width	length	top	bobbin	foot	feed dog	comments
hemstitching	wide	10–12	universal		presser	in place	wing needle
cut work	0	0	universal		darning	lower	use hoop
machine needle-weaving	1–4	0	universal		darning	lower	use loosely woven fabric

ADDITIONAL IDEAS

■ Work this chapter's design in a flat panel of transparent fabric. Hang in a window framed by plexiglas.

■ Insert a small lace or hemstitched heart on the bodice of an evening dress.

■ Make a room divider of scrim in which selected areas have been machine needlewoven.

■ Sew free-form cut work shapes on silk organza and back with a vibrantly colored fabric. Insert into the sides of a square or circular lucite plant holder.

■ Work a rectangle of yellow hemstitching on transparent fabric and satin stitch this in the form of "August" to red transparent fabric. Cut away the excess hemstitching and work cutwork circles in the corners of the red before appliquéing to your fabric calendar. (You tend to skip the ends of chapters, don't you—see Chapter 2—Additional Ideas.)

TEN
⊙RDINARY MATERIALS FOR PATCHES

GLOSSARY

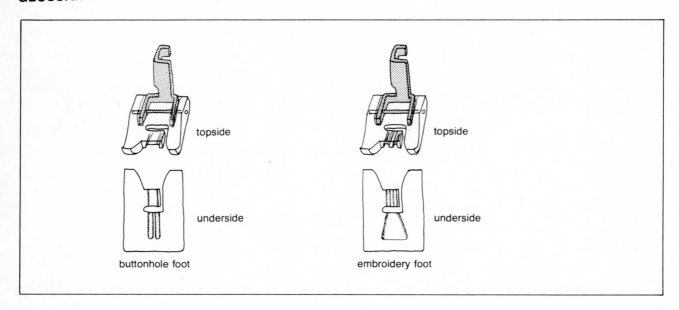

topside

underside

buttonhole foot

topside

underside

embroidery foot

THE TECHNIQUE

Now that you've learned a passel of techniques and special machine stitchery effects, you're ready to apply all this knowledge in a variety of ways on the different fabric scraps you hoard.

In this chapter, after learning how to handle small bits of fabric, our project will be to make several 3″ (7,5cm) circular patches, to be sewn to jeans, jackets, purses, hats, quilts, etc. These make quick, easy, and attractive gifts and sell well at boutiques and craft fairs. However, instead of ending this chapter with how-to

Plate 40

directions as in previous chapters, I'll sprinkle the how-to's through the text. Whether or not you intend to make a particular patch, the directions cover the handling of knits, special edges, and other valuable information you may need to know for your own projects. All of the patches are pictured in Color Plate 4. (Plate 40)

In choosing fabric for patches to be worn, remember to select machine-washable, colorfast threads and fabric.

Since the best-looking work is done when the fabric is stretched, we will use a hoop for all these projects. But suppose the fabric you want to use is smaller than the hoop—how do you handle it?

The Rainbow Patch (Diagram 62) began with a small, irregular piece of pillow ticking perfect for sky, but it wasn't as large as the 3″ (7,5cm) circle patch. First I cut a piece of lightweight cotton (left over from the Mexican peasant blouse) 2″ (5cm) larger around than my hoop, and mounted the fabric into the hoop (the top of the hoop with the screw goes under the fabric, remember—see Chapter 4). On this backing fabric in mid-hoop, I traced around a wide-mouth pint canning jar with a pencil. You could also use a protractor to draw the circle. Laying my small piece of pillow ticking over the sky part of the circle, I pinned it to the backing fabric. At this point some of my guidelines

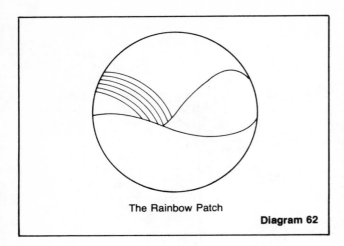

The Rainbow Patch

Diagram 62

were obscured, so I again traced around the jar, lining up with those previously drawn and extending the circle onto the pillow ticking. You could also stitch around your pencilled circle at the onset of a project so that you'd always have a guideline visible on the back.

Removing the presser foot, I then put the hoop under the needle, put on the embroidery foot, and machine-basted around the edges of the pillow ticking, using my fingers to keep the fabric from puckering. (Diagram 63)

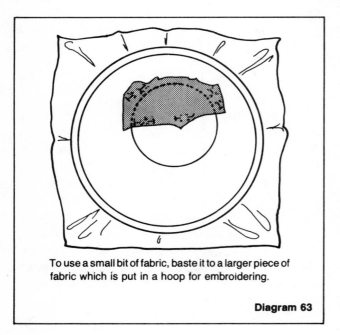

To use a small bit of fabric, baste it to a larger piece of fabric which is put in a hoop for embroidering.

Diagram 63

I drew guidelines for the rainbow and set up my machine for satin stitch, using the embroidery foot. Since I did not have a doodle cloth, I second-guessed tension settings, based on the notes I jotted down for earlier work. I loosened both top and bottom tensions one notch. While I had to change top thread several times, I didn't bother to change the kelly green bobbin thread. I stitched the rows of encroaching zigzag, starting outside the circle and extending them below the hill. The grooves on the underside of the embroidery foot helped the foot move easily over the previous rows of satin stitch.

As I finished each row, I lifted the presser bar lever, gently pulled some thread through the take-up lever, moved the fabric to the left side of the needle, and cut the top thread. Without changing the bobbin thread, I returned to the top of the second row of the rainbow, changed the top thread color, held the thread end securely as I lowered the needle into the fabric, and stitched the second row, which covered the loose bobbin thread on the back. The ends of top thread were later covered by the appliqué hills. (Diagram 64)

I traced the hill on the right side of the design onto tissue paper, pinned the paper to some green fabric and cut out a hill, leaving a ¼" (6mm) margin all around. Then I clipped the margin and pressed it under (but didn't bother with parts that would be hidden—I pressed only the curve of the hill). I pinned the hill to the circle and put a piece of blue net over it (optional, but it suggests the way the hills look in the distance). With a straight stitch on the machine (don't forget to change tension settings on your machine when changing from one type of stitch to another), I applied the hill to the circle, afterward cutting off the excess net close to the stitching. Every time a portion of the circular guidelines was covered up, I redrew it so as not to lose them. Next I changed thread color to white, top and bottom, and satin stitched around the circle once. Taking the fabric out of the hoop, I cut close to the edge of the circle, and satin stitched again, using my fingers to make the fabric behave. I guided the cut edge under the center of the foot so that the needle actually went once into the material and once outside. Last, always, I pressed.

Incidentally, for all satin stitches, begin stitching at the side or bottom of the patch, rather than the top, so that the eye of someone looking at your work is not

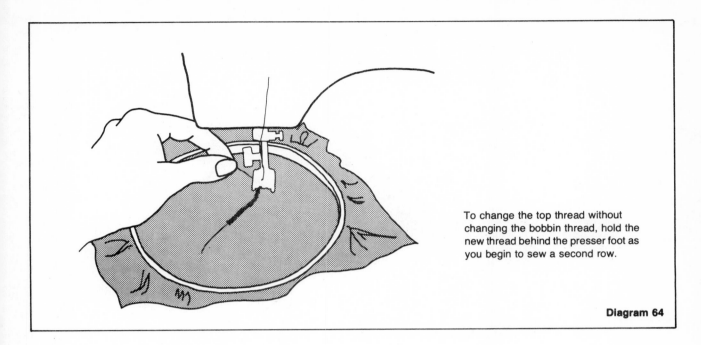

To change the top thread without changing the bobbin thread, hold the new thread behind the presser foot as you begin to sew a second row.

Diagram 64

drawn to those starts and finishes. (Diagram 65)

Some people do not pin and machine-baste their appliqué shapes to a backing, preferring instead to join the two fabrics with fusible webbing. On the same principle, other sewers cut plastic grocery bags smaller than the appliqué shape and then fuse the appliqué to the backing. I prefer the first method, as it's less risky for the iron.

Handling a zigzag on stretchy fabrics like jersey and knits is sometimes difficult until you learn the simple trick explained in *The Flower Patch* (Diagram 66). Two other ways to avoid stretching knits are first, to back

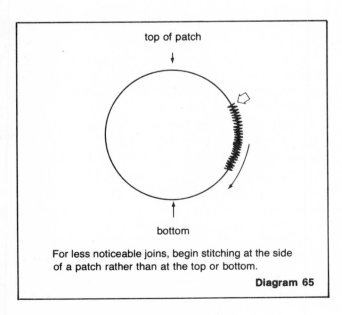

top of patch

bottom

For less noticeable joins, begin stitching at the side of a patch rather than at the top or bottom.

Diagram 65

The Flower Patch

Diagram 66

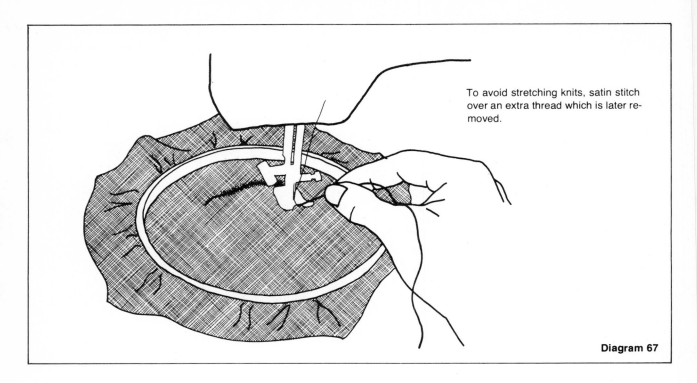

To avoid stretching knits, satin stitch over an extra thread which is later removed.

Diagram 67

the fabric with interfacing or typing paper, so it won't stretch badly when you put it into the hoop. The other, if possible on your machine, is to decenter the needle to the left, which makes the stitches more regular on tricot, jersey, and other knits.

Here is another quick project, *The Flower Patch*, which utilizes a small hand embroidery motif that was an advertising hand-out in a can of coffee, proving that someday, somehow there will be a use for all those silly little scraps you save. Copy the design onto tissue paper and free machine baste it directly to a rectangle of yellow knit, backed with interfacing or typing paper, and mounted in a hoop. Tear off the tissue paper when the cartoon has been transferred. Free machine embroider the pansies with zigzag shading from the outside of the petals into the middle, using two shades of purple and a yellow center. Use a free machine straight stitch to add the stems and leaves.

Now for the trick to handling stretchy fabrics. Set up the machine for zigzag with the presser foot, loosening top and bottom tensions slightly. Set the stitch length at 10-12 stitches per inch to make an open zigzag. Hold

another piece of sewing machine thread on top of your fabric on the seam line, over which you will zigzag. Hold the extra thread slightly taut, but not so hard you pull it out. This extra thread prevents the fabric from stretching (Diagram 67). Take the fabric out of the hoop, cut close to the edges, press with a damp cloth, and then remove the extra thread by pulling gently. Now set the stitch length for closely spaced zigzag, and satin stitch the edges, using your fingers to the sides of the presser foot to guide the material evenly into the machine.

A good way to practice monogramming is by making a *Name Patch* (Diagram 68). Choose a medium- to heavyweight fabric that can withstand a lot of satin stitch pulling at its threads (burlap would not be good, but denim is perfect). Put the fabric into the hoop and write your favorite person's name (all right, write your own name) in pencil. Use white pencil, chalk, or wax if the fabric is dark. Since the tension must be perfect for monogramming, practice on a doodle cloth in the hoop first. If you wish, lower or cover the feed dogs. Take off the presser foot and put on the darning foot. Set the

Name Patch

Diagram 68

patch. Remove the patch from the hoop, cut close to the edge, and satin stitch again. Press from the back.

For an extra-special edge on a patch, try the one I used on my *Symbol Patch* (Diagram 70). Use the same procedure to mount fabric in a hoop and to trace a circle that we have been using for all the patches. Use any symbol meaningful to you or your organization. I filled in this symbol with silk buttonhole twist in

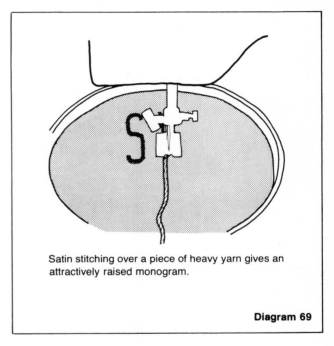

Satin stitching over a piece of heavy yarn gives an attractively raised monogram.

Diagram 69

stitch length at 0 and do not set a zigzag width yet. I used an extra-fine variegated pink cotton thread in the top and white in the bobbin. Extra fine sewing machine thread will make your monograms more precise and neater. I also stitched over a piece of rug yarn to raise the monogram slightly. Draw up the bobbin thread and lock the first stitch, cutting off the end threads. Now set the machine to whatever zigzag width you prefer (I like the third widest setting). The line you drew should be in the middle of the zigzag as you work. Let the machine run quickly to make a neat satin stitch, but move the frame slowly and steadfastly. Don't stop turning the frame until you finish a letter, or the monogram will look uneven (Diagram 69). At the end of each letter, raise the needle, set the zigzag to 0 for both width and length and take a few stitches in one place to lock the threads. Now raise the presser bar, pull some top thread through the take-up lever, and gently pull to the side until you can clip the top thread. Don't worry about the bobbin thread—most of it will be covered by satin stitch, and the remaining parts can be cut off since all stitches are locked at the beginning and end of each letter. Start the next letter by lowering the needle into the fabric, taking a few stitches in the same place to lock threads, setting the zigzag width, and stitching as before. Decorate the outer rim of the patch any way you want—I used one of my decorative cams in lime green and satin stitched around the outside of the

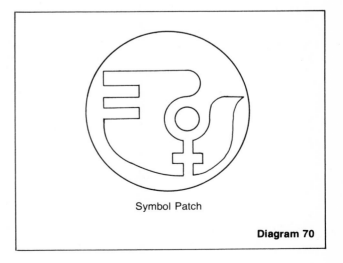

Symbol Patch

Diagram 70

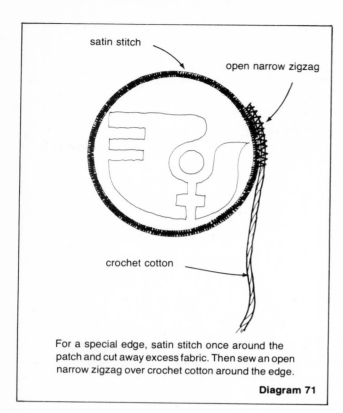

satin stitch

open narrow zigzag

crochet cotton

For a special edge, satin stitch once around the patch and cut away excess fabric. Then sew an open narrow zigzag over crochet cotton around the edge.

Diagram 71

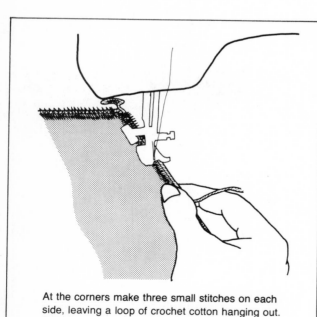

At the corners make three small stitches on each side, leaving a loop of crochet cotton hanging out. Return to an open narrow zigzag. Stop machine with the foot down and pull the crochet cotton gently until the loop disappears.

Diagram 72

encroaching satin stitch on wool, with a loosened upper tension and a Size 14 (90) needle. I backed the wool both with organdy and with typing paper, as so much zigzag on a soft fabric can badly distort the fibers. If your satin stitch looks wobbly in places when finished, consider cheating as I did—threading a tapestry needle with the silk floss and filling the gaps with either hand satin stitch or backstitch.

Now for the special edge, satin stitch the edge with a wide zigzag (I changed to extra-fine cotton for this and I almost forgot to change my Size 14 [90] needle to a regular Size 12 [80]). Remove the hoop and cut off excess material close to the stitches. Set your stitch length to 10-12 stitches per inch and your stitch width to a narrow zigzag. Lay a piece of 3- to 5-ply crochet cotton or any thick thread along the edge of the patch and zigzag over it, taking care that the cord stays exactly at the edge. (If you only have a thinner crochet cotton in the house, double the cord.) The embroidery foot on some machines has a small hole in the front through which you can feed this cord. I found it helpful to hold this strand slightly above the front of the embroidery foot so that the cord was guided into the right-hand groove of the embroidery foot (Diagram 71). You will have a hanging loop if you start a doubled strand of crochet cotton at the top of the patch, leaving as much loop as you need to hang the patch on a tree or wherever you hang patches. Finish by threading the two cut ends into a tapestry needle and sliding them under the satin stitch on the back.

If you were using this cording on a square piece of fabric you would zigzag to within 1/8″ (3mm) of the corner, set the stitch length to 0, and hand turn the wheel to make three stitches, leaving the needle in the inside edge. Raise the presser bar and turn the work. With your left finger make a loop with the cord, lower the presser foot, and make three more stitches by hand. Now set the stitch length back to 10-12 stitches per inch and zigzag for a few inches. Stop the machine, leaving the foot down, and gently pull the cord from in front of the foot until the loop you made at the corner disappears. Push the six corner stitches toward the point with a pin until they are arranged evenly. When you reach the place where you began, cut off the cord, and overlap the satin stitch about 1/2″ (1,3cm). (Diagram 72)

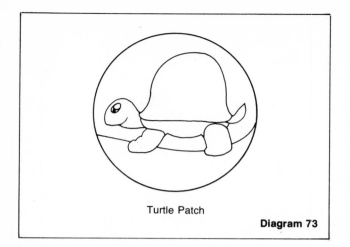

Turtle Patch

Diagram 73

the back, tie off the crochet cotton with the sewing machine thread. Tear off the typing paper and don't worry about the remaining part covered by the ground stitching. (Diagram 74)

Take off the hoop and turn the fabric over, so the topside faces up. Lay a piece of yellow knit fabric or felt over the circle. On tissue paper, trace the shape of the turtle with a felt-tip pen. Pin the tissue paper to the yellow fabric, lining up the ground with what you've just worked. Set up the machine for free machine embroidery: darning foot on, sewing machine cotton thread in top and bobbin, loosened tensions top and bobbin, stitch length 0, stitch width 0, fabric in hoop. Pull up the bobbin thread and lock the first stitch. Then free

I used another kind of edge, similar to this one, on my *Turtle Patch* (Diagram 73), which is slightly stuffed and made of non-washable fabrics, since it is to be sewn on my backpack and will not be subject to the wear and tear of a patch on jeans, for example.

Start by winding No. 5 brown pearl cotton onto a bobbin and setting the bobbin tension to 0. Use cotton sewing machine thread on top, with a tight upper tension (8 or 9—try it on a doodle cloth first). Put a rectangle of lightweight blue cotton backed with organza into the hoop, with the underside up. From the design trace the circle and slope of the ground onto typing paper with felt-tip pen and then pin this paper to the underside of the fabric, turning the paper over so the design will appear the right way on the topside. (You'll be able to see the felt-tip line on the underside of the paper.) Using the embroidery foot and a medium stitch length (10-12 stitches per inch), sew once around the circumference of the circle, starting at one side of the horizon. Now fill in the ground by stitching back and forth, watching the previous line of stitching in the slot of the presser foot. The rows of stitches should be very close together. When you've filled it in completely, raise the presser bar lever and gently pull the fabric to the side of the needle. Cut off threads, leaving generous tails. Thread a tapestry needle and pull the crochet cotton to the back. If you have missed filling in any places and the background blue shows through, use this thread end to make small hand stitches. Then on

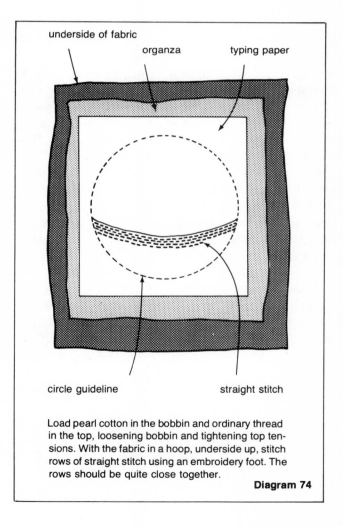

underside of fabric

organza   typing paper

circle guideline   straight stitch

Load pearl cotton in the bobbin and ordinary thread in the top, loosening bobbin and tightening top tensions. With the fabric in a hoop, underside up, stitch rows of straight stitch using an embroidery foot. The rows should be quite close together.

Diagram 74

machine embroider the outline of the turtle, using small stitches. Lock the last stitch and cut the ends. Remove the fabric from the hoop and tear off the tissue paper with tweezers. Then cut the yellow fabric close to the line of stitching, taking care not to cut the background fabric or the couched brown threads of the ground. I like to use cello-tape to pick up the clipped threads and small pieces of lint.

For the shell, put a square of green velour onto a piece of organza. Copy only the turtle shell shape onto tissue paper with a felt-tip pen and pin the pattern to the velour. Your machine is already set up for free machine embroidery, so you can do the next step without a hoop or presser foot if you feel confident enough. Otherwise, put the presser foot on. Stitch right through the tissue paper, ⅛″ (3mm) inside the turtle shell pattern. Turn the shell over and with your seam ripper or a pair of scissors, carefully cut a slash in the organza—but not through the velour. Push some stuffing (old nylons, cotton, or Dacron batting, whatever you have) through the slash and spread it evenly throughout the shell, using the eraser end of a pencil for a poker. Don't stuff the shell too full, and push towards the front, so the back will lie flat. You may sew up the slash by hand, but it isn't absolutely necessary. Trim the organza close to the line of machine stitching. Then cut along the shell outlines, through the tissue paper, velour, and organza.

Put the backing fabric into the hoop again and pin the green shell over the yellow turtle. Set up the machine for free machine embroidery, as above, and quilt the shell to the background, following first the outline and then adding the lines of the shell.

Finally, the special edge. Keep the hoop under the needle, but put on the buttonhole foot. This foot has grooves underneath to accommodate two parallel lines of satin stitch (or use an embroidery foot). If you wish, use extra-fine sewing machine thread in the top (I used the rayon I love so much). You have already laid a line of pearl cotton around the circle, so satin stitch over it as in the *Symbol Patch* above. I found it helpful to decenter the needle to the left, so I could control exactly where the needle entered on each side of the crochet cotton. Use a small zigzag width, just big enough to cover the cord (Diagram 75).

Take the fabric out of the hoop and cut close to the

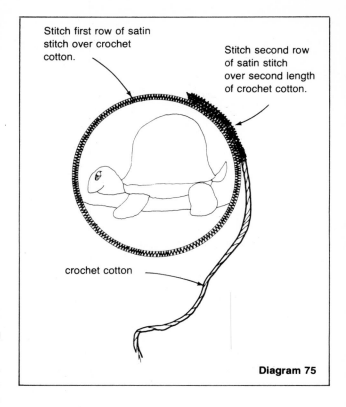

Diagram 75

first line of stitching. Now decenter the needle to the right. Widen your zigzag and lay another line of crochet cotton to the right of the first one. This should fit exactly into the second groove of the buttonhole foot and the zigzag should be wide enough to cover both the second cord and the first line of stitching. Satin stitch all the way around the circle. Isn't that a beautiful edge (after pressing, of course)?!

The *Jeans Patch* (Diagram 76) shows you how to handle points, curves, and scallops with satin stitch. Trace the design onto tissue paper and pin to the back of your background fabric. Put rectangles of red and blue fabric larger than are needed onto the topside of the white fabric. Put the fabric into the hoop, underside up. Stitch once around the circle; this circle of stitches will be used later as a cutting guide. Straight stitch or zigzag with a narrow width around the diamond and heart shapes. The reason you work from the back and then cut out the shapes is that trying to satin stitch fussy little shapes to a background could easily drive you nuts. Take the fabric out of the hoop and carefully

Jeans Patch

Diagram 76

The inside top point of the heart is like a scallop. Since the needle is decentered to the left, stitch until the left side of the needle hits the imaginary vertical center of the heart. The right side will have gone beyond the center. With the needle in the fabric, lift the presser bar lever and pivot the material counterclockwise. Move the stitch width lever to 0, lower the presser bar lever, and take a few stitches. Then slowly increase the zigzag stitch width, as if you were filling a wedge shape, reaching with your needle and zigzag width for the imaginary vertical center line. (Diagram 78)

The point at the bottom of the heart and the points of the diamond are handled in a way similar to the scallop. This can be done either with the needle decentered or not. If the needle is not decentered, start decreasing the zigzag width about ⅛″ (3mm) from the

cut away the excess red and blue fabrics. Using a zigzag width larger than the narrow one you used to secure the fabrics, satin stitch around the heart with the needle decentered to the left. You could use a decorative stitch in place of the satin stitch.

To handle the curved corners at the top of the heart, stop the needle on the inside of the curve, lift the presser foot, and pivot the material a minute amount. Lower the presser foot, take another satin stitch, and let the needle go into the same inside hole. Continue this procedure until you are around the curve. (Diagram 77)

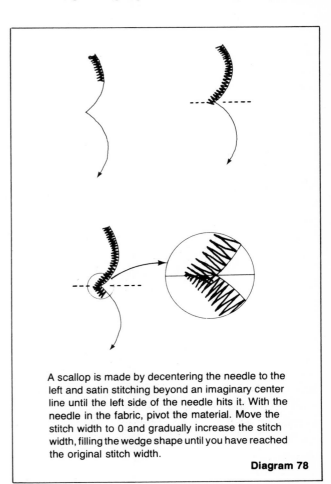

A scallop is made by decentering the needle to the left and satin stitching beyond an imaginary center line until the left side of the needle hits it. With the needle in the fabric, pivot the material. Move the stitch width to 0 and gradually increase the stitch width, filling the wedge shape until you have reached the original stitch width.

Diagram 78

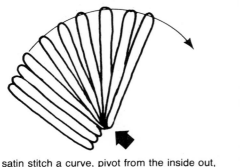

To satin stitch a curve, pivot from the inside out, returning the needle to the same hole on the inside edge. For each stitch leave the needle in the fabric, raise the presser bar lever, and pivot the material slightly.

Diagram 77

Ɗo's . . .

- ■ find inventive uses for all those fabric scraps you hoard
- ■ baste small fabrics to a backing big enough to fit in your hoop
- ■ select machine-washable, colorfast threads and fabrics for wearable patches
- ■ use a hoop whenever possible
- ■ begin satin stitching edges in an unnoticeable place

AND DON'TS

- ■ forget to reset your machine for ordinary sewing
- ■ stop turning the frame in the middle of a monogram

point. At the point, with the needle in the fabric, pivot the material and reverse the order of what you just did, increasing the zigzag width back to what it was. If you have a vari-width lever or dial, use it.

To sew patches to garments, I often sew one row of satin stitch, cut out the circle, and then secure the patch to the clothing with another row of satin stitch. If I've taken the time to sew a super edge, I set up the machine for free machine embroidery and sew patch to garment with an invisible line of straight stitch along the inside edge of the satin stitch. Some people prefer to hold the patch to the backing by bonding with a fusible web before stitching.

ADDITIONAL IDEAS

■ Choose any of this chapter's designs, blow them up, and work them on selected blocks of a child's quilt, interspersing the designs with rectangles of fabric in bright crayon colors.

■ Cut fabric petal shapes, work the special edge of the Symbol Patch over flexible wire, and bend them into shape.

■ Monogram your pillow case as described in the Name Patch.

■ Blow up the Rainbow Patch design and work it on the back of a denim jacket.

■ Superimpose "September" over a solid background of zigzag shading, leaf shapes, fall colors. (Trace around real leaves if you can't draw.) Work everything *but* the letters "September." (Catch up with the rest of us by reading Chapter 2—Additional Ideas.)

ELEVEN

NUSUAL FABRICS

GLOSSARY

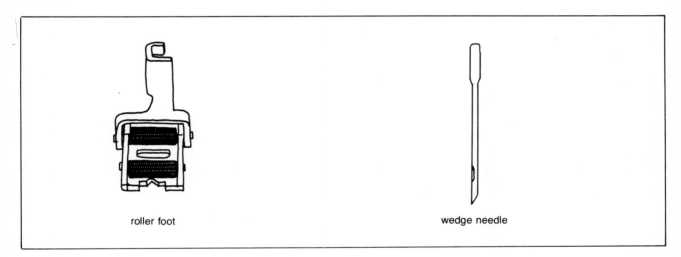

roller foot

wedge needle

THE TECHNIQUE

By now you realize that any fiber system is fair game for machine embroidery. Anything that is woven, knit, poured, or crushed together to make a surface through which a needle will pass can be explored for its potential in machine embroidery. Naturally, some of your attempts will be unsuitable for anything but the wastebasket, but some will be both usable and striking.

Felt is a material especially well-suited to machine stitchery because it, too, works up fast. And its bright colors are cheerful to sew on. All of the machine stitchery techniques covered in the book look attractive on felt because the sewing thread lies on the surface of the fabric, with no background weave competing for attention.

However, I have always been somewhat annoyed at the claims that satin stitch on felt is easy. Until I learned to use extra-fine thread and to loosen both top and bobbin tension, my attempts at satin stitch on felt looked terrible. Appliquéing felt to felt requires machine basting with either a long straight stitch or a long zigzag before working the satin stitch. Use lots of finger control to keep the felt from moving around too much. If your fabric store does not carry a 50% wool felt, check with an interior decorator. Felt, of course, is not washable, so use it for items that will be drycleaned only.

I learned an interesting treatment for felt from artist/author Jean Ray Laury. Using the thinner felts of 75% rayon, she tears shapes with pliers, which treatment gives a soft, fuzzy edge. This is then stitched to a background with free machine embroidery. (Plate 41)

Another edge treatment is to cut down the middle of a piece of felt with pinking shears, which produces a sawtooth pattern on both edges. Separate the two edges about 3″ (7,5cm) apart and appliqué them to a lighter or darker backing of felt. Apply a piece of rickrack trim down the center of the 3″ (7,5cm) gap and secure it with a narrow automatic stitch. The serrated edges of the trim complement those of the felt.

See-through plastics also adapt superbly to machine stitchery. These are available in various weights at hardware stores. The medium-weight pliable plastics are easiest to work with. Don't pin anything to plastic because the pin holes remain. For the same reason, you can't afford to make mistakes. cello-tape designs to the plastic and sew right through the paper and tape, pulling both off when you're finished. The automatic stitches are magnificent, worked on see-through plastic; however, if the plastic is not strong and the needle holes are allowed to pack too closely together, the plastic will rip. (Plate 42)

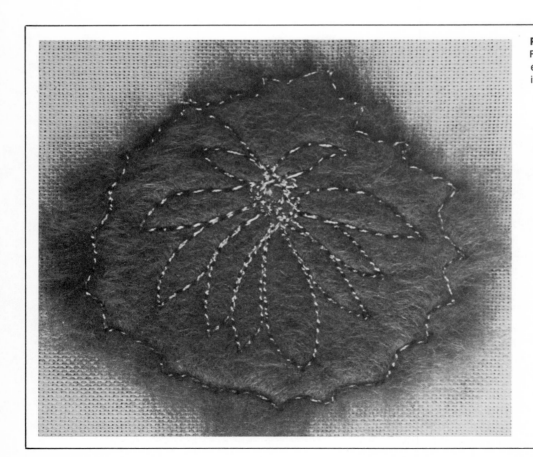

Plate 41
Fuzz felt by pulling at the edges with pliers or ripping it instead of cutting.

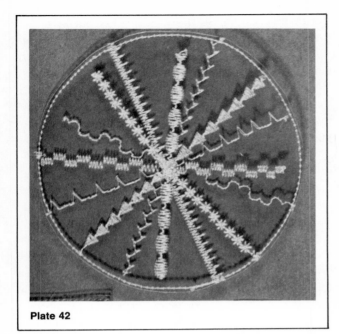

Plate 42

Because plastic has body and is weatherproof (except for long periods in the sun which cause it—and me—to deteriorate), it is the ideal fabric to cover and protect other fabrics. The project at the end of this chapter is decorations for an outdoor living Christmas tree.

Occasionally when stitching on plastic, friction builds up between the bottom of the presser foot and the fabric, causing the plastic to stick. Use a roller foot to prevent this. I also use the roller foot for leather and imitation leather, and for some knits.

Vinyl can be found in the form of a colored plastic backed with cloth, which makes it easier than clear plastic to sew on. The automatic stitches, in particular, work up very nicely on vinyl, with the threads lying evenly on its smooth surface. I haven't upholstered a car in vinyl and automatic stitches yet, but . . . .

Most industrial manufacturers ship their fragile wares in an amazing variety of plastics and foam, many of which can be stitched on. I've experimented with substituting plastic for batting in machine quilting. Of course the ultimate use of the article you are making determines whether or not you use plastic. I would not put an item with plastic incorporated into it

into a hot washing machine, for example. On the other hand, I once made a fabric greeting card for a friend in which I backed some crêpe-backed satin with a small piece of ⅛″ (3mm)-thick opaque flexible plastic. (I don't know what to call the plastic because I filched it from a wastebasket in my husband's company.) I free machine embroidered my friend's name through the crêpe/plastic/muslin, which quilted it and brought the surface into relief. This particular plastic, pliable yet not limp, would adapt well to free standing objects, such as small, soft boxes.

I can imagine a see-through plastic raincoat which is pintucked over colorful heavy cords—but would the coat be waterproof with all those needle holes in it?

Sewing on leather requires a special wedge needle to make a big enough hole in the fabric. There are many kinds of leather, some of which are too thick to sew on. The leather stripping sold in fabric stores for belting can be applied as trim to garments, using automatic stitches along the edges to secure the leather to the fabric. Again, as with plastics, don't pin the leather—tape it. I have seen a gorgeous leather purse worked from the underside with a crochet cotton in the bobbin, laying a thick chain stitch on the surface (so far, only a few domestic machines can do this stitch).

Sewing construction on leather is different from that on ordinary fabrics. I suggest you consult a good sewing book, of which my favorite is EVERYTHING ABOUT SEWING LEATHER AND LEATHER-LIKE FABRICS (from Vogue Patterns).

The new imitation suedes are also beautifully enhanced by any kind of machine stitching. As with other nonwoven fabrics, the sewing thread lies on the surface instead of being swallowed by a weave. The rubber backing of these fabrics sometimes shreds rayon thread, but cotton thread works superbly. Free machine embroidery without a hoop on imitation suedes is not easy because the underside of the fabric sticks to the bed of the machine, but backing with typing paper eliminates some of the problem. Actually, I prefer automatic stitches with the roller foot to free machine embroidery on these fabrics. Tensions must be loosened slightly to prevent rippling, and after stitching, the fabric should be pressed from the back with an iron set to the manufacturer's temperature suggestion.

To prove how nuts I am about machine embroidery,

I've even tried stitching on Dacron batting and raw fleece. Both must be backed with organza, to keep the woolly bits from being drawn into the bobbin case, but it works. I recently made a mass of fluffy clouds outlined and formed by satin stitching. I haven't yet stitched through foam or fur, but only because I don't have any in the house.

However, there is a knit-backed imitation fur that adapts beautifully to machine stitchery. Use the knit on the outside for a vest or coat, turning the fabric back on itself at all facings for a fur trim. Then use any of the machine embroidery techniques to embellish the coat front, backing the fabric with typing paper to prevent the fur from catching in the bobbin. (Diagram 79)

Terry cloth can be difficult to stitch on because the loops catch on the needle and presser foot, and yet monogrammed or appliquéd towels can lend such a personal touch to your home. To cope with this, copy your design onto a rectangle of organza and pin the organza to the right side of the towel. Put the fabric into a hoop and set up the machine for free machine embroidery with the darning foot on, stitch length on 0, stitch width at whatever you like, extra-fine thread in the top and bobbin. Run the machine fast but move the hoop slowly and constantly for an even monogram. If you are an accomplished sewer, use a tapered satin stitch at the beginning and end of the monogram. When you have finished, cut the organza as close to the satin stitch as possible. Then use your handy tweezers to remove any threads of organza that are sticking out unattractively. This same method can be used to appliqué a fabric to towelling. Place the appliqué on a larger piece of organza which is pinned to the towel. Put the fabric in a hoop and satin stitch around the shape. Then cut away the organza and pull out excess threads with the tweezers. (Diagram 80)

I plan to experiment with glass fabrics soon. Although they are not yet suitable for apparel, being too irritating to the skin, glass fabrics make beautiful curtains, and occasionally, bedspreads. I would imagine that whip stitch worked on glass curtains would lend an intriguing shadow effect as the sun passes through.

I have experimented with automatic stitches on No. 12 needlepoint canvas, and some of the automatic stitches look enchanting, but I haven't yet figured out how to use my experiments. As mentioned in Chapter 9, bands of automatic stitches on ribbon can be padded and applied to the borders of canvas work.

Cross-stitch embroidery uses a backing called (appropriately) cross-stitch canvas, similar to penelope canvas. This is basted to fabric, stitches are worked across the intersections, and finally the threads of the canvas are withdrawn one by one and discarded. This technique can be duplicated with zigzag by carefully matching the length and width of the stitch to the canvas so that the needle never actually pierces a canvas thread, and by matching succeeding rows of zigzag exactly, to resemble cross stitch. Using a limited color palette and choosing patterns that have solid blocks of stitches, you can come up with a passable cross stitch. I am not averse to adding isolated hand cross stitches to fill out the outskirts of the pattern. (Plate 43)

Upholstery and drapery stores carry some fascinating open-weave fabrics that can be embellished in interesting ways. One is to withdraw threads as if you were checking for the straight grain. Then set up the machine for free machine zigzag and pull the exposed threads together with satin stitch. Another way is to

Turn the fur on knit-backed furs to the topside for a self-trim. Then decorate the fur.

Diagram 79

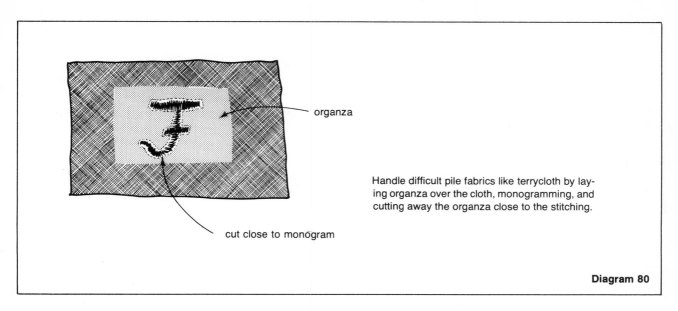

organza

Handle difficult pile fabrics like terrycloth by laying organza over the cloth, monogramming, and cutting away the organza close to the stitching.

cut close to monogram

Diagram 80

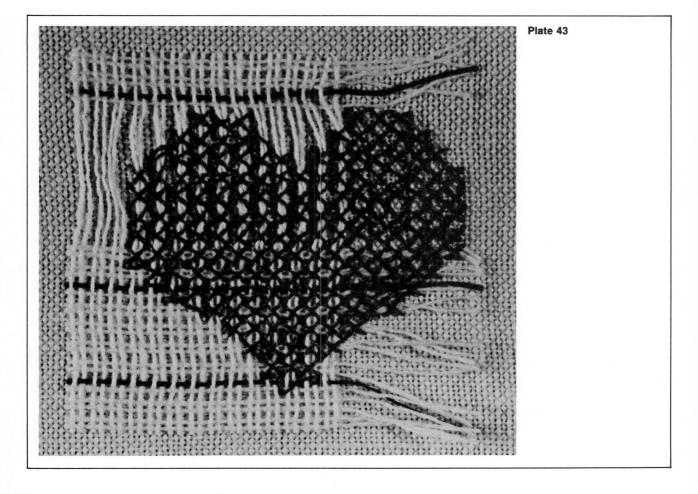

Plate 43

Do's . . .

- experiment on all fabrics
- use organza to subdue the loops of terry cloth

AND DON'TS

- pin plastics

---

withdraw threads as above, and work automatic stitches along the top and bottom edges of the exposed threads. This combines well with hand stitches, gathering the threads as in drawn thread work.

The last two unusual fabrics that I've decorated are used mainly for whimsy. I often free machine embroider messages to friends on interfacing and have also used it to make tags for presents. Likewise, I've stitched small pictures on typing paper to send in letters to people I enjoy surprising.

I haven't tried stitching on flower petals or rainbows, but only because there hasn't been an opportunity.

CHRISTMAS TREE DECORATIONS

(pictured in Color Plate 4)

A fast and attractive way to try some of the unusual fabrics is to make decorations for an outdoor living Christmas tree. The decorations will be protected from weather by a casing of see-through plastic (available at hardware stores).

you will need:

1 yd. (0,95m) of see-through plastic
bits of felt, organza, nylon stockings, linen, etc.

assorted threads
your imagination

Snowflake step-by-step:

1 On a piece of typing paper, draw a 4″ (10cm) circle. Divide it in half with a straight line and divide that straight line in half with another straight line. Divide each of those in half with straight lines. The circle now has twelve equal parts. (Diagram 81)

2 Load any color thread in the machine. I used silver. Use a roller foot if you wish.

3 Put a square of plastic over the typing paper. Starting at the center of the intersecting lines, stitch automatic patterns out, using all the ones you have.

4 Gently tear off the typing paper and cut the plastic into the shape of a snowflake.

5 For a quick hanging loop, lay a piece of string or crochet cotton on a piece of typing paper. Satin stitch

over it in any color. The paper will tear off easily. Loop the string and satin stitch the ends to the plastic.

Christmas Tree step-by-step:

1 On a rectangle of green felt, draw a Christmas tree. (Diagram 82)

2 Load the machine with yellow extra-fine rayon and set up the machine for vari-width zigzag. Loosen tension slightly. Stitch a line of Christmas lights as shown, using red rayon on the second string of lights.

3 Fold the tree in between plastic and cut the sides of the plastic to make a triangle. Stitch an automatic or free machined star at the top of the tree right through the plastic. Stitch with any color thread around the triangle. Hang by the method described in Step 5.

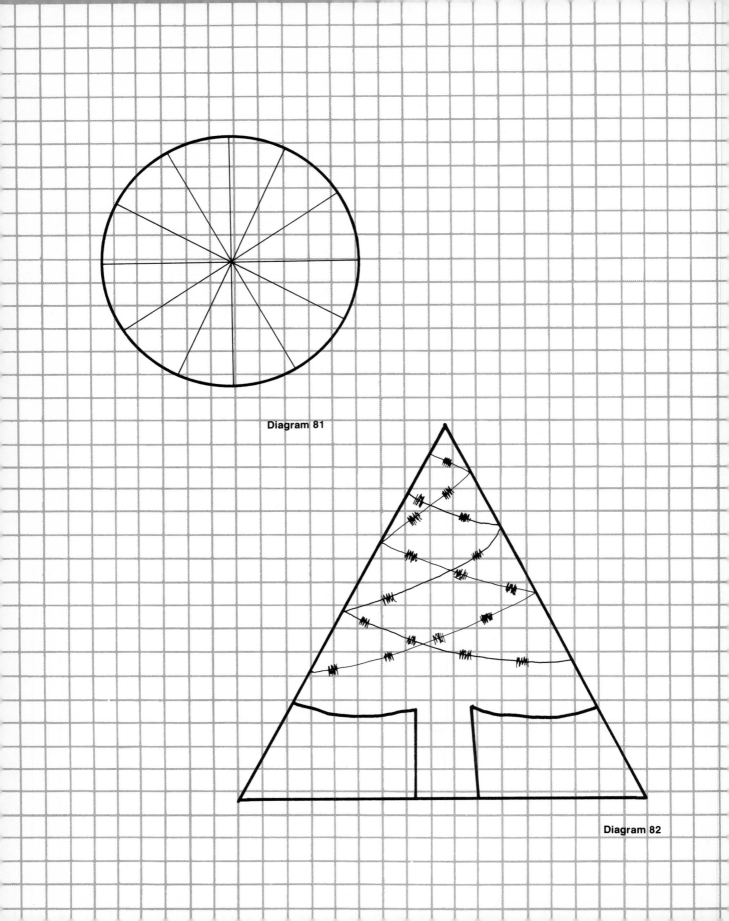

Diagram 81

Diagram 82

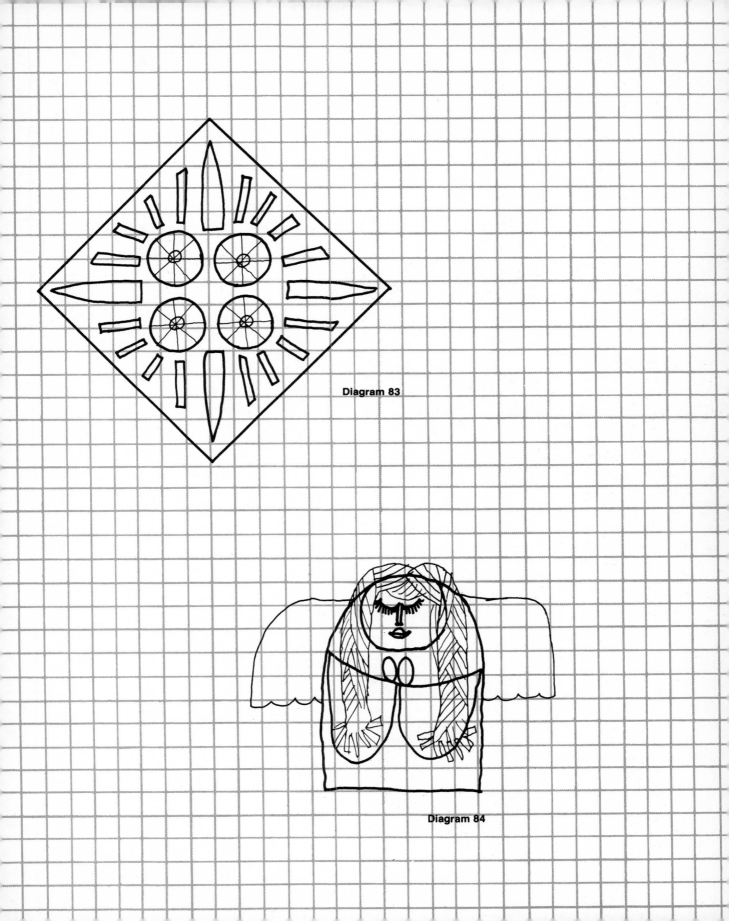

Diagram 83

Diagram 84

Cut Work step-by-step:

1 Put a piece of white organza (or finely woven linen or wool or whatever you have) into the hoop. Work four cut work circles as shown on the cartoon (Diagram 83) with extra-fine white thread. Work lines of encroaching zigzag plus zigzag shading to fill the other shapes, leaving the center slit unworked. When finished, slit the centers with a seam ripper. If desired, picot the edges of the organza.

2 Cover the cut work with an envelope of plastic, straight stitch around the edges, and make a loop.

Angel step-by-step

1 Cut two pieces of white fabric in an arch as shown in the cartoon (Diagram 84). Right sides together, sew the curved side ¼" (6mm) seam. Turn and press lightly. Press under the bottom seam.

2 Gently push a small amount of Dacron batting into the fabric envelope.

3 Set up the machine for free machine embroidery: darning foot on, stitch width 0, stitch length 0, black thread above and below. Free machine quilt the angel's hands and close the bottom edge by stitching near it.

4 Cut about 4" (10cm) from a tube of nylon stockings. Open out flat. Lay the stocking on a rectangle of glazed Dacron batting (back with organza, if you wish). Free machine embroider the face. If you don't feel secure enough to try it unaided, trace the face onto tissue paper. Stitch right through the tissue paper onto the stocking. Then gently tear away the tissue paper with tweezers.

5 Pad the back of the face with a small wad of Dacron batting and gather the stocking behind the head. Stitch it together and cut off any excess nylon.

6 Put a bunch of yarn hair over the head, hiding the back of the head. Hand stitch it in place.

7 Lay the body of the angel on a piece of plastic. Lay another piece of plastic carefully over the body, taking care not to squish her. Copy the shape of the angel's wings on a piece of typing paper and lay it under the bottom piece of plastic. Follow the lines in a straight stitch all around the wings and body. Tear away paper and trim close to the stitching.

8 Hand tack the head to the plastic and make a hanging loop.

Name Mobile step-by-step:

1 Cut the name of a friend out of red felt.

2 Cut rectangles of plastic to fit around each letter.

3 Lay the felt envelopes on a piece of typing paper in a vertical line, separating each letter by 2" (5cm). Tape the envelopes in place.

4 Starting at the top, sew a straight stitch all the way around. Then sew from the middle of the bottom edge of the first letter to the middle of the top edge of the second letter.

5 Sew all around each block in this manner and then gently tear away the paper and tape.

6 Fashion a hanging loop.

ADDITIONAL IDEAS

■ Make a stacked felt wreath enclosed in a large plastic pocket to hang outside in any weather.

■ Embellish a knit-backed imitation fur coat with Celtic motifs (see page 187—Bibliography) laid down in couching-by-piercing.

■ Pintuck see-through plastic over colorful cords to make a raincape.

■ Make a vinyl bean-bag chair with ornate lines of automatic stitching as topstitching.

■ Free machine embroider an orange stocking-face pumpkin (dye the nylon) to be used as the O in "October" of your fabric calendar. Free machine embroider the rest of the letters in black. (Not a trick—treat yourself to Chapter 2—Additional Ideas.)

TWELVE
PRINTED FABRICS

THE TECHNIQUE

Most of the designs we've attempted so far have been solid colored threads on top of one-color fabrics, but machine stitchery on printed fabric opens up a whole world of possibilities.

The easiest of this type of stitchery is machine-quilting a printed fabric (Plate 44). Striking designs in wide widths can usually be found in custom drapery stores, but if you can only buy 45″(115cm)- or 54″ (140cm)-widths, a seam can be made invisible by matching patterns exactly. If you are working on a quilt-sized piece, you generally do not have any left-over material on which to practice, so it is extremely important to practice free machine quilting on a trial sandwich of similar fabric/stuffing/backing material. You must pin liberally and loosen both top and bottom tensions slightly, so that when you begin quilting, the material does not move around and make ugly puckers. To handle recalcitrant fabrics that fight even the most skillful pinning job, put a piece of typing or adding machine paper between the needle plate and the fabric, gently tearing the paper away after quilting.

To free machine quilt, set up your machine for free machine embroidery, removing the presser foot and lowering the feed dogs (optional). As usual, I use the darning foot and sometimes a hoop. The hoop is both a help and a hindrance. If your pattern is large, you will have to move the hoop several times before completing an outline, which is a nuisance—but on the other hand, you waste so much time ripping out mistakes if you don't use a hoop, that the inconvenience becomes minor.

Take your time in maneuvering the hoop so that your stitches will be comparatively even. You can even challenge the legendary 12-16 stitches per inch of old-time quilters by moving the hoop slowly as you stitch and by putting the foot pedal on slow speed (if possible on your machine).

Usually you'll have repeated patterns or motifs to quilt. When you finish one motif, raise the presser bar lever and pull some upper thread loose above the needle. Then gently move the material away from the needle to the next starting point, changing the hoop position if necessary. Lower the needle into the fabric, lower the presser bar lever, and hold the extra thread behind the needle. Take several stitches in the same place to lock the thread and later cut off the loose threads on the front and back. They will not pull loose because you locked them. This saves you tying off a million threads as you go. If you doubt whether the threads will last through several washings, you can pull the upper thread through to the back and tie additional knots or use a drop of fabric glue on the back.

Plate 44

You need not always think in terms of large projects like quilts, though. Here is a 12″ (30,5cm)-square batik handkerchief, purchased at a craft fair for under $5, which has been backed with muslin with a lightweight flannel interlining, quilted on the main outlines in a contrasting color, cut down the center, and assembled into a striking yet simple tunic top. Quilting tie-dyed fabric gives a similar effect. (Plate 45)

A favorite fabric to embellish for its ready-made straight lines is pillow ticking or any striped fabric. You can stitch on the lines, between lines, zigzag over lines, or if you're feeling energetic, you can completely cover the lines. Checked or gingham fabric is also fun to embellish, as the basic shapes are already there for you to play with. (Plate 46)

Likewise polka-dot fabrics are easily arranged into a larger pattern, although it can be frustrating to have a picture in your mind of a particular fabric and then to search all over town in vain for it. Again, large graphic fabrics are often found in drapery stores and the weight of these fabrics is perfect for free machine stitchery without a hoop.

Don't be afraid to create your own patterns if you can't find what you want. There are several fabric paints on the market, available in art and craft supply stores (or see Supply List), which can be used straight from the bottle. You want really large polka dots? Assuming you've already removed the sizing by pre-shrinking the fabric, merely pour some paint into a dish, dip the bottom of a flat juice glass or bottle top into the paint, and press onto the fabric. Re-ink the glass and print until satisfied. Let the paint dry and then set the colors as directed by the manufacturer. Presto!, you have your own printed fabric ready for embellishment. (Plate 47)

Be careful that your hours of machine work on printed fabric are not wasted by choosing a thread color or weight that is lost on the fabric. For example, I once started some lettering on dress-weight linen that was quite weak and ineffectual because the thin lines of extra-fine sewing machine thread were swallowed by the thicker threads of the linen. I ended up using silk floss.

Color is also important. In choosing to decorate with machine embroidery, we choose to emphasize a particular area, so select a color that stands out—either

Plate 45
Close-up of batik fabric quilted to emphasize the lines of the design.

Plate 46

Plate 47
Like your polka dots heart-shaped? Carve a heart on half a potato and print on fabric, putting newspaper underneath to soak up excess.

the strongest color in your print or one that is complementary. I once stitched a bold red design among large green and white polka dots—and it worked!

Have you ever tried combining prints to make a new fabric on which to stitch? The juxtaposition of print on print when colors have been carefully coordinated can be very exciting. Joyce Whitcomb-Black of Portland, Oregon, carries the idea of using many printed fabrics even further by collecting fabrics printed with realistic pictures, cutting them up, and reassembling them into fantasy scenes. She says, "I use a variety of cotton and cotton-blend fabrics, all pre-shrunk, cotton lace trims for the gingerbread houses, black for wrought-iron fences. I spend hours every week checking my local fabric stores for neat prints, textured fabrics, laces, etc. I call my work Appli-Tique and it's done with the zigzag on a Singer Golden Touch & Sew. I use mercerized cotton thread only. I find poly-thread stretches and tangles on my machine. I use lots of the large dressmaker pins with glass heads to hold the material securely while I zigzag using lots of finger control to keep the tucks and excess fabric in place." (Plate 48)

You can also combine solid-covered fabrics to make a new surface on which to stitch. For example, I once made an evening bag divided in half vertically by black and white silk, which I then stitched in white on the black side, and black on the white. (Diagram 85)

Another way to make your own fabric is to sew strips of lace and ribbons together (backed with lining fabric), interspersed with strips of machine embroidery, either with automatic cams or any of the textured stitches discussed earlier in the book.

Machine embroidery can be combined with a different kind of "printed" fabric, canvas work (also called needlepoint), for a truly unusual look. I have worked bands of automatic stitches on grosgrain ribbon which are sewn to the unworked canvas border with more

Plate 48
Appli-Tique by Joyce
Whitcomb-Black

automatic stitches. I lay flannel on the canvas for padding to bring the ribbons to the height of the canvas work. It is important to design carefully, though, and plan from the beginning to use machine embroidery with the main design; otherwise the results can be unsatisfactory.

It is challenging to lift part of a pattern off a fabric and to enlarge and embellish it, as pictured (Plate 49). Sometimes the design of a fabric or trim can be picked up for another part of the garment. I recently made a halter dress with an attached black organza cape. On the cape in white thread, free machine embroidered, I duplicated the swirls of the skirt fabric pattern. I've also taken the pattern off white eyelet lace used as sleeves, enlarging and satin stitching it on the bottom edge of a child's dress.

In embellishing these extensions of prints, you may want to add beads. If you're sure the hole in the bead or sequin is large enough for the needle, you can

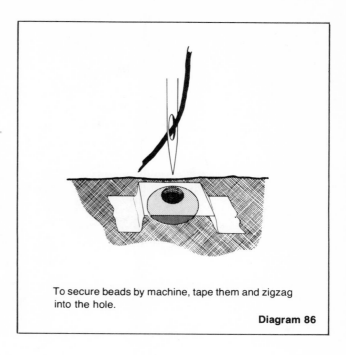

To secure beads by machine, tape them and zigzag into the hole.

Diagram 86

machine sew them on by cello-taping them to the surface and carefully stitching with the darning foot. (Diagram 86)

Another aspect of embellishing prints is to borrow one motif from a pattern. Cover it completely with solid stitching, zigzag or straight stitch, except for the outer ⅛″ (3mm) of the motif. Cut out the embroidered motif and appliqué it to a garment, jacket, shirt, dress, purse, or pillow, by satin stitching the remaining ⅛″ (3mm) of outline. (Plate 50)

Although the method called machine smocking is really machine gathering, it can be used successfully on printed fabrics with regular pattern repeats, which are used as guidelines in stitching. Hand wind elastic thread onto the bobbin, taking care not to stretch it. Load embroidery or sewing machine thread in the top and tighten the upper tension slightly. The longer your stitch length, the more pronounced will be the gathers. Use adding machine or typing paper under the material to hold it in place, tearing the paper away later. If you plan well, you may vary the overall shape of your smocking area to further imitate the feeling of hand smocking. You can also use a decorative stitch that alternates from side to side of a middle line, and by

Diagram 85

Plate 49

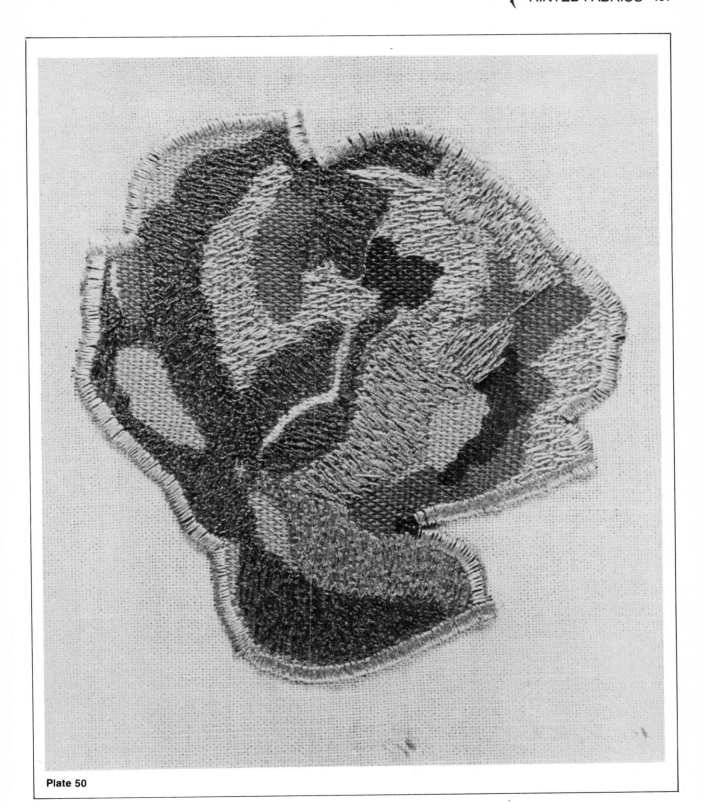

Plate 50

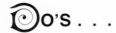

Do's . . .

- ■ prevent puckers on slippery quilt fabrics by backing with adding machine or typing paper
- ■ print or construct your own prints

AND DON'TS

- ■ waste hours of machine time by choosing a thread color or weight that does not show up on the backing

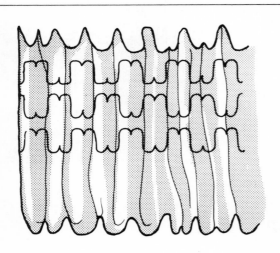

Use your decorative stitches with machine smocking (gathering) to create a striking effect.

Diagram 87

carefully locating the line-up of stitches, create an elegant effect. (Diagram 87)

Work the smocking first and then cut out the garment. Allow the material below the smocking area to remain gathered and lay the pattern piece over the smocked material. If you were to pull the material out flat, the garment would be too small at the bottom and not hang right.

One unusual use of machine-embellished fabric is to glue it to any household object—not just recipe boxes and wastebaskets, but the telephone, the dining room chairs, your sewing machine! It's really quite easy to do; you need a fabric glue like Elmer's, a razor blade, scissors, and patience mixed with whimsy. If the back of your fabric is lumpy with threads, bond iron-on interfacing to it. Then paint your object liberally with glue and carefully smooth the fabric onto its surface, molding the fabric into hollows and over bumps. Cut slashes for anything that protrudes and trim excess neatly with the razor blade.

Color plate 1 Sampler of Machine Embroidery Techniques

Color plate 2 Bread Board Apron and Butterfly Sunshine Dress

Color plate 4

Patches
Sewing Machine Cover
Christmas Decorations

Color plate 5

Flower pillow
Americana Handbag

Color plate 3 Mexican Peasant Blouse

Color plate 6   His & Her Caftans

Color plate 7   Tunic and Hat

Color plate 8   Pat Shipley, "Pineapple"

156

Color plate 9 Judy Lewis, "Rainbow Painter"

Color plate 10
Riccar instructor,
"Kabuki Dancer"

Color plate 11
Joan Schulze,
block from machine
embroidered quilt

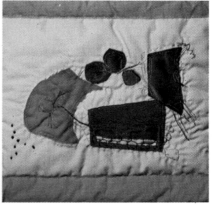

Color plate 12 Jo Reimer, close-up of firescreen

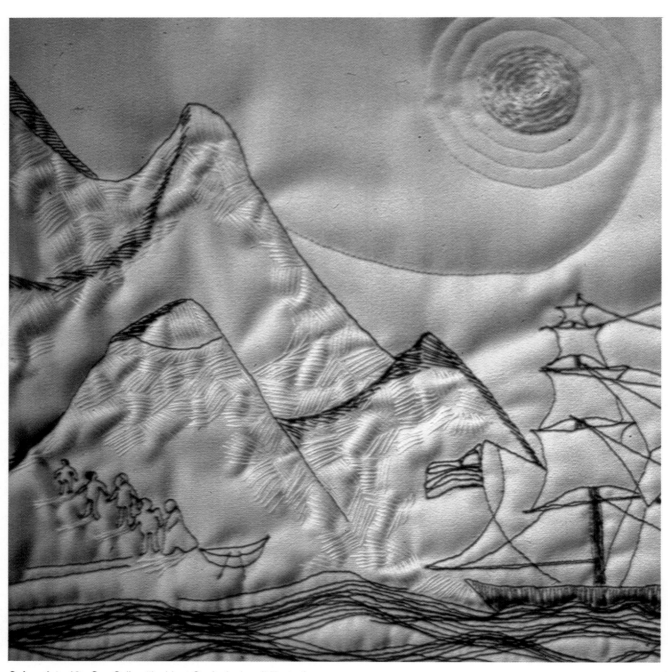

Color plate 13   Sas Colby, "Incident On An Iceberg" illustration

ᗷUTTERFLY SUNSHINE DRESS

(pictured in Color Plate 2)

The children's dress calls on your skills in satin stitch, appliqué, free machine embroidery with a hoop, and free machine embroidery without a hoop, with a heavy thread in the bobbin worked from the underside. All these skills—and you can still finish it in an afternoon!

you will need:

10″ (25,5cm) square of white lightweight cotton fabric

10″ (25,5cm) square of lightweight interfacing

white 100% cotton thread

white No. 5 pearl crochet cotton

embroidery hoop, embroidery and darning feet, scissors, pins

tracing paper and pencil

doodle cloth for white appliqué polka-dot fabric

doodle cloth for polka-dot fabric

polka-dot yardage appropriate to your children's pattern

pattern with no front seam

step-by-step:

1 Place the tissue paper over the cartoon (Diagram 88) and trace the circular form and butterfly shape onto it. Cut around the circular form. Now cut out the butterfly wings carefully with scissors or razor blade.

2 Pin this circle to the white fabric and trace around it with a pencil. Trace the missing butterfly wings too. Remove tissue paper.

3 Machine-baste the interfacing to the back of the white fabric and put both into the hoop, as you learned in Chapter 4.

4 On your doodle cloth, which has also been backed with interfacing, determine the best setting for satin stitch on your machine. I loosened top and bottom tensions slightly. Don't forget to label directly on your doodle cloth. You may need this information again.

5 If your machine is like mine, you will have to take off the embroidery foot, put the hoop under the needle, and then put the embroidery foot back on. Do so.

6 Using a satin stitch, go around the circle once. Then stitch around the butterfly wings once with a narrow satin stitch, starting at the bottom of the wing and following the arrows on the cartoon.

7 Remove the hoop from the machine and from the material, and cut out the circle close to the zigzag

Diagram 88

stitches. Press. With a pair of sharp pointed scissors, cut out the butterfly wings as shown, leaving the center body intact.

8 Cut off the excess tissue paper from your dress front pattern piece. Pin the pattern to your fabric and trace around it with a white pencil or tailor's chalk.

9 Cut in a rectangle around the pattern, leaving generous margins, for easier free machine embroidery later.

10 Pin the satin-stitched circle to the front garment wherever you like, lining up the grain of the white fabric with the grain of the dress fabric. If you don't pin liberally, you will probably growl when the fabrics start to tango.

11 Stick the hoop back on and machine-baste the circle to the fabric. Remove pins. Satin stitch over the previous satin stitches on the outside circle.

12 Leaving on the hoop, take off the presser foot and put on the darning foot. Starting at the center body, pull up the bobbin thread and lock the first stitch.

13 Embellish the printed fabric that shows through the butterfly wings in whatever way strikes your fancy. I've circled the polka dots and scalloped the edges of the wings. Be careful when you cross the heavy satin stitch on the way to the other wing—it will be difficult for your needle to penetrate all those stitches, so proceed slowly here. Take the hoop off the machine and material.

14 Wind white pearl cotton onto the bobbin. Bypass bobbin tension when you load it into the machine.

15 Working from the underside so that the pearl cotton is laid onto the surface, fiddle around with your polka-dot doodle cloth until you find the correct tension.

The pearl cotton should not be pulled through to the top (which in this case is the underside), so the top tension should be loosened slightly.

16 Trace the rays of the sun onto typing paper and pin directly to the underside of the fabric, matching the circular forms to line up everything evenly.

17 Holding the fabric in both hands as shown in Chapter 5, move the fabric slowly in free machine embroidery, being careful to keep the fabric near the needle flat against the needle plate as each stitch is taken, so it won't pucker (the darning foot and typing paper also help). Gently tear off the typing paper. Tie off the first and last stitches on the underside.

ADDITIONAL IDEAS

■ Blow up and use this chapter's butterfly sun on a large floor pillow.

■ Tie-dye and free machine quilt a bedspread.

■ Make a carrying bag for needlework of heavy pillow ticking covered in selected places by rows of your favorite machine embroidery techniques.

■ Construct a telephone book cover by sewing ribbons, lace, and strips of automatic stitching to a fabric backing.

■ Work the word "November" in rust-colored canvas work (needlepoint), surrounded by a cream canvas work background. Lay a border of automatic stitching on ribbon onto the canvas and raise it to the level of the canvas work by padding with flannel. Your fabric calendar is almost done (last chance to see Chapter 2—Additional Ideas).

THIRTEEN

GALLERY

The challenge of machine embroidery is to explore its unique language of texture and color. Presented in this chapter are several artists who express themselves via the techniques discussed earlier in the book. Whenever possible, specific information is given on how they achieved their results. Although brands of machines are named, this is not intended as an endorsement of any sewing machine.

Pat Shipley, of Palo Alto, California, studied light falling on a pineapple. She drew the pineapple on muslin and quilted it with a straight stitch presser foot on, using an older model of Pfaff (no zigzag, no decorative stitches). She then covered the padded areas with light and dark fabrics, straight-stitched on, and placed organza and other materials for the leaves. (Color Plate 8 and Plate 51)

Judy Lewis, of Lake Oswego, Oregon, explains her work. "I primarily use appliqué, using a Singer Touch and Sew, and make use almost exclusively of the zigzag to cover raw edges of the fabric. I use mostly medium to heavy cotton/polyester blends, such as Trigger. I do use free-motion embroidery and the machine works wonders making waves, swirls, and eddies. The rainbow design (Color Plate 9 and Plate 52) is filled with a pre-quilted bedspread remnant and backed in a solid color which comes around as a border on the front. I have also done about a dozen

designs on the backs of denim workshirts. I buy the shirt, take out the back panel (ugh), do the appliqué, and then put it back together. It's a pain to do, but they're really neat and so nice for men (and women) to wear." This wall hanging is also used with a pre-quilted piece. (Plate 53)

Working in free machine embroidery, Sas Colby, of Berkeley, California, has created an illustration for INCIDENT ON AN ICEBERG (Color Plate 13 and Plate 54) by Mary Ellen Chase (Houghton Mifflin, unpublished). Sas did the original drawing on muslin and then padded the muslin with quilt batting backed with white sailcloth. She worked on a Sears' Kenmore, dropping the feed dogs. After free machine stitching from the muslin side, she turned the piece over. Thus the bobbin thread became the thread we see. Hand stitching was also added for more texture.

An instructor of the Riccar-Tokyo Company created the Kabuki Dancer (Color Plate 10 and Plate 55), which was later applied to a plate. Each area of color is achieved by a marvelous color blend of Japanese rayon embroidery thread, accented by gold and silver metallic threads. The Riccar machine is adapted by dropping the feed dogs, decreasing top and tightening bobbin tensions, using a small needle (Size 10/11 [70]), removing the foot, and stretching the fabric in a wrapped hoop. Much of the filling-in is done with tapered zigzag moved side to side and slightly forward in a long-and-short stitch.

Jo Reimer, of Portland, Oregon, uses heavy threads (pearl cotton, fine wools, six-stranded embroidery floss, etc.) in the bobbin of her Bernina and stitches from the underside to lay these threads on the surface. She suggests that those people owning machines with detachable bobbin cases, such as hers, use a second bobbin case marked with nail polish for machine embroidery, so the tension screw can be changed without worrying about resetting it. Pictured is part of a fire screen (Color Plate 12 and Plate 56) which was worked from both the topside, using free machine embroidery to stitch down the layers of sheer fabrics, and underside to lay the heavier threads.

Robbie Fanning, of Menlo Park, California, used the automatic stitches on her Elna to create a rainbow. The illusion of hills and windows on the buildings was created by vari-width zigzag. Silk organza was doubled, and building shapes, a piece of crochet, and an angel were sewn to the inside. The haiku celebrates the beginning of California's rainy season and says, "Gray city tosses rainbow magnet over hills—magic! brown becomes green." (Plate 57)

Joan Schulze, of Sunnyvale, California, uses transparent fabrics and free machine embroidery to achieve colors and lines that flow gently into each other. She says, "I use the sewing machine as a drawing tool. It is a free feeling, as I can design as I work. Many times I feel as if the machine and I are one, just like someone else might feel with pen, pencil or crayon. I also use it for emphasis and embellishment, pushing this to its limits (not the usual guide book instruction). This combines with hand techniques to achieve effects I would need years to get totally by hand, if at all." Pictured here is "Not So Secret Garden," done on an Elna, and Color Plate 11 is a color close-up of one block from a free machined quilt. (Plate 58)

Combining free machine embroidery and see-through plastic is a jellyfish by Madge Copeland, of Sunnyvale, California. She works on a Singer, putting a plate over the feed dogs and allowing the bobbin thread to loop freely. (Plate 59)

In another use of plastic, Madge has created a Family Portrait, enclosing felt in plastic. (Plate 60)

Eleanor VandeWater, of Vancouver, Washington, uses many different kinds of fabrics in her work —velveteens, suede cloth, velours, knits, and linen, among others. Pictured is a stole owned by the Gethsemane Lutheran Church, in Portland, Oregon, which says, "And the word became flesh and dwelt among us." (Plate 61)

Plate 51 Pat Shipley, "Pineapple"

Plate 52 Judy Lewis, "Rainbow Workshirt"

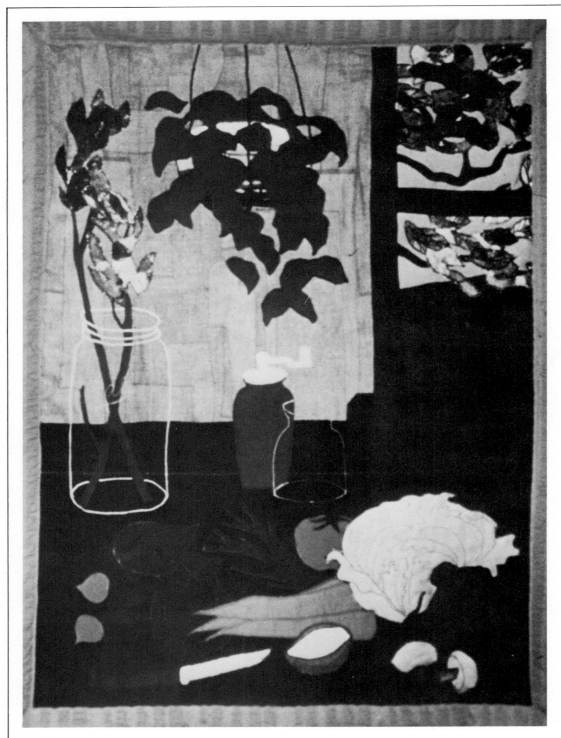

Plate 53 Judy Lewis, "Kitchen Wallhanging"

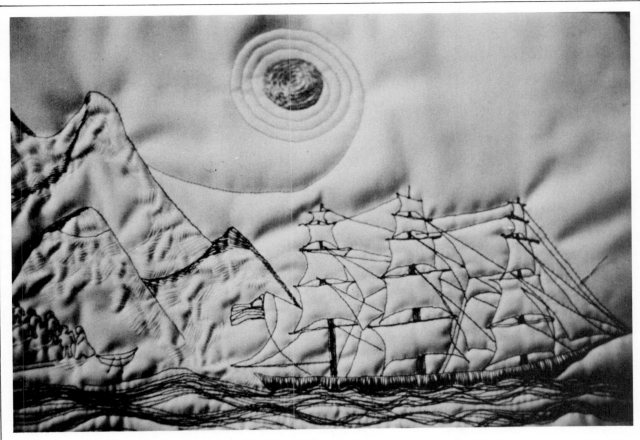

Plate 54 Sas Colby, illustration for INCIDENT ON
AN ICEBERG

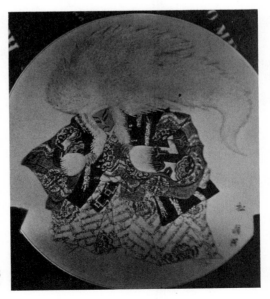

Plate 55
Riccar instructor, ''Kabuki Dancer''

Plate 56 Jo Reimer, close-up of firescreen

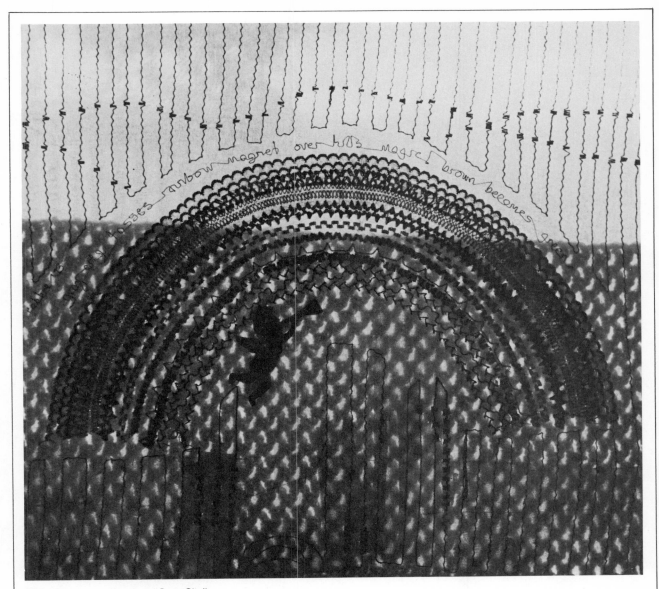

Plate 57 Robbie Fanning, "Gray City"

Plate 58 Joan Schulze, "Not So Secret Garden"

Plate 59
Madge Copeland,
"Jellyfish"

Plate 60
Madge Copeland,
"Family Portrait"

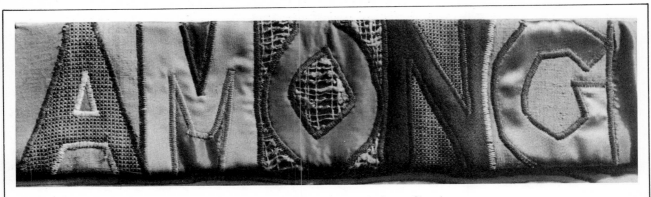

Plate 61 Eleanor VandeWater, close-up of stole owned by Gethsemane Lutheran Church

FOURTEEN

ADAPTING DESIGNS AND DEVELOPING YOUR OWN

At this point your head is stuffed with wonderful dreams of machine embroidery. You know the possibilities inherent in each technique and the wide range of exciting fabrics waiting for you to embellish.

But now it's time for you to strike off in your own unique direction. Where can you find designs and how can they be adapted to machine embroidery?

The easiest designs to translate into machine stitchery are hand embroidery designs, particularly iron-on transfers. Your aim, though, is *not* to sew a machine-embroidered garment trying to pass as a hand-embroidered one. Machine stitchery has its own proud look—so change the designs any way you want to make them look right for what your machine can do. Generally hand-embroidered stitches fall into these general categories: detached, continuous line, and filling. The table on page 177, MACHINE INTERPRETATION OF HAND STITCHERY, lists the types of hand stitchery and suggests alternatives on the machine.* (Plate 62)

Don't forget that a combination of hand and machine embroidery can be beautiful.

Here's the process I followed to develop a hand embroidery iron-on transfer (Diagram 89) into machine embroidery. (Color Plate 7)

*If you've forgotten what a particular stitch is and how to do it, see the handly all-at-one-glance machine embroidery chart on p. 188.

The pattern showed a white tunic top embroidered in navy blue, but it would be boring and not highly visible to machine embroider in one dark color. Instead I chose a backing fabric of a navy blue cotton/polyester blend of medium weight to withstand the stress of all that embroidery pulling at its threads (especially the heavy zigzag). (Plate 63)

I was in a hurry to make the garment and almost did not preshrink it. *This is a modern world,* I thought. *Surely we don't need to pre-shrink fabrics anymore.* True, the fabric did not shrink—but it bled all over the washer. Can you imagine the pain of putting hours of machine time on a stunning garment, only to have it bleed all over the embroidery the first time you washed it?

Naturally I did not follow my own advice about doing the work *before* cutting out the garment, so lots of teeth-gnashing resulted when I tried to put a hoop onto the small shoulder areas. Instead, I should have cut off the excess tissue paper from the pattern piece, pinned the pattern to the fabric, traced around with white pencil or tailor's chalk, and cut out a large rectangle of fabric. Oh, when will I ever learn?

Now I positioned the iron-on transfer on the front, double checking to be sure it lined up correctly, and followed the directions for transferring the pattern onto my fabric. The transfer had a small flower motif in one corner to be used as a test sample. I transferred this

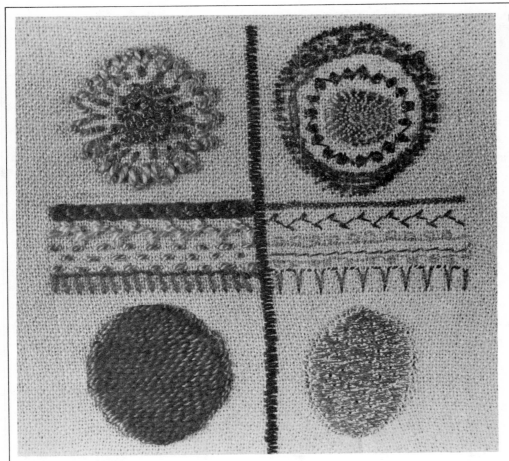

Plate 62
On the left are hand stitches. On the right are some machine interpretations. The left side took more than twice as long to work as the right.

MACHINE INTERPRETATION OF HAND STITCHERY

hand stitches	machine stitchery interpretation
Detached-seeding French knot, detached chain (lazy daisy)	These can be a pain in the neck, involving the tying off of millions of threads. If you can possibly link the detached stitches together, do. A design that calls for French knots in the center of a flower, for example, can be worked in a spiral of whip stitch or cable stitch. If you cannot replace a detached hand stitch and do not want to eliminate it entirely, either work a whip stitch and carefully remove the top thread, bonding the back so the loops won't pull out, or work separate satin stitch spots.
Continuous line (includes most hand embroidery)— chain, running (stem, back stitch, et al), cross, cretan, fly, buttonhole, herringbone, etc.	These can be simplified into beautiful rows of plain old straight stitch, particularly if you use a variety of colors. If you have decorative cams, use them liberally when the lines of the design are broad and sweeping (rather than angular, which would drive you nuts to work). You can also load thick (washable, if it's a garment) thread in the spool and work a couched or free machine embroidered line. Almost all of the techniques covered in the book can substitute for continuous line hand embroidery.
Filling-satin and chain are used the most	Either free machine zigzag or free machine straight stitch can fill a space. If possible use a hoop; otherwise back the fabric with typing paper or interfacing. You can also (1) machine appliqué fabric to replace hand filling stitches; (2) work cut work separately and then appliqué to shapes; or (3) trapunto and pad the shape.

Diagram 89

Color Code:
a   yellow
b   pink
c   orange
d   red
e   light green
f   dark green

Plate 63

onto a doodle cloth. Because my fabric was medium weight, I did not back it with interfacing, but I wish I had—the extra body helps the fabric withstand heavy machine embroidery.

I began by embroidering the stems and leaves in free machine embroidery (pattern called for outline and chain), using a Spanish rayon thread, darning foot, and hoop. Every line was traced over several times (same as we did on the Mexican peasant blouse in Chapter 6), both to cover up the lines of the iron-on transfer and to make the design more visible. Instead of taking the fabric off the hoop or cutting threads as I finished each section, I simply moved the hoop. When I ran into the flower heads, I stitched along a transfer line, down a petal, around to the center, and out another petal to the next stem, planning to cover these lines later with satin stitch.

Next I worked the satin stitch on the petals. I put the doodle cloth into the embroidery hoop and tested encroaching zigzag on one petal. Once I had the tensions loosened slightly, it seemed to work fine, so I tackled the garment, putting the fabric in the hoop (and keeping it on for all the flowers).

Because the fabric was stretched in a hoop, it retained its shape without puckering . . . but the satin stitch pulled the centers of the flowers out of whack. (You wouldn't notice unless I told you, though, so don't tell anybody.)

I probably should have covered the feed dogs (or lowered, if that's your way) for this heavy satin stitch, since the threads on the back occasionally snagged slightly, but I'm so used to free machine embroidery with the darning foot only, that I didn't bother. Instead of changing threads as I worked the flowers along the border, I worked all the reds first, then all the pinks, then all the oranges. Your first attempt will be the worst, so don't start with the one in the middle where everybody looks first. You don't need to change the bobbin thread—I used red for all flowers—but start with a full bobbin. It's irritating to run out halfway into a flower.

It took me about two hours to work the front of this tunic. Should you pause halfway through, don't leave the hoop on the fabric overnight. Loosen the screw or take the hoop off entirely.

I really should have worked the straight lines first since they are sometimes pulled slightly out of kilter by heavy zigzag. At the neck I used a line of red straight stitch, a line of decorative stitching in orange where the pattern called for running stitch, another line of pink straight stitch, and another line of decorative stitching in yellow where the pattern called for herringbone. If your cam stitch is not the same on each side, decide which should face the center of the tunic.

Last I filled in the scroll shapes at the bottom in free machine embroidery with the hoop on, moving it along as I worked, as I did for the leaves and flowers.

In the search for design you can learn from ready-made clothes too. When I recently visited a Mexican import shop, I jotted down some ideas for edging machine embroidered clothes, based on hand embroidered blouses—e.g., using a decorative cam for scalloping at the edge of the neck and sleeves, zigzagging over a few strands of twisted crochet cotton or embroidery floss, about an inch in from the sleeve, and then pulling and tying it to gather the sleeve edge. This particular blouse was on the rack, but I have also been known to follow people around, sketching their clothing for my idea file. (Diagram 90)

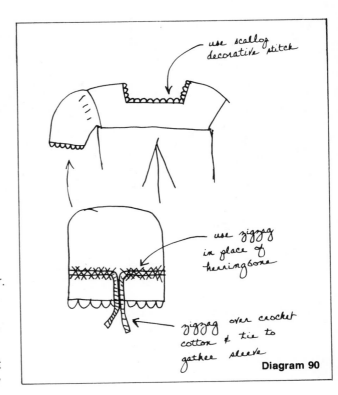

use scallop decorative stitch

use zigzag in place of herringbone

zigzag over crochet cotton & tie to gather sleeve

Diagram 90

Plate 64

As for developing your own designs, don't panic. People sometimes have a mistaken idea about design originality—"But I can't!" they gasp, looking at the advanced examples in the gallery section. Of course you can! . . . if you start with a simple design and learn where to look for ideas. It isn't as if you have to stare at a blank sheet of paper and suddenly come up with the World's Greatest Design. There are many people and places you can consult in developing your own machine embroidery ideas.

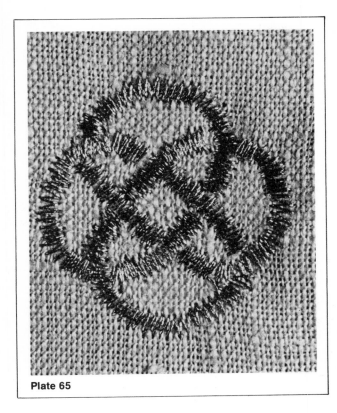

Plate 65

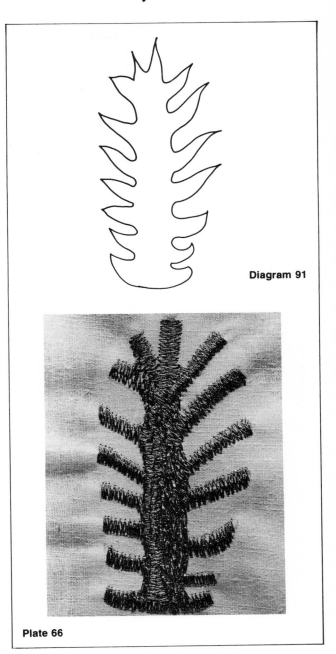

Diagram 91

Plate 66

Actually the design from almost any needlework technique can easily be adapted to machine embroidery—patchwork, canvas work (needlepoint), knitting, etc. Here is the traditional patchwork pattern called "Log Cabin" worked in the traditional method—i.e., assembling components of a geometric design—but instead of using plain and patterned cottons, I've used organdy worked in cut work with lace insertions over taffeta. The idea is the same but the language is all machine embroidery. (Plate 64)

Another ready source of designs can be uncovered by exploring the 700 (Dewey Decimal) or N (Library of Congress) section of your public library. Not only are there many general books of design motifs used throughout the history of the world, which designs are easily adaptable to various machine embroidery techniques, but there are literally thousands of books showing specific cultural or art media designs. To illustrate, here is a knotwork motif from CELTIC ART (see Bibliography) which I adapted for satin stitch. (Plate 65)

When you are adapting designs, don't be afraid to toss out the most complicated lines in favor of simplicity and to change shapes freely to fit your own likes and dislikes. The points on leaf tips done in satin stitch drive me crazy, so I often round them off. (Diagram 91 and Plate 66)

While you're at the library, poke around in the natural science section for those gorgeous big picture books of flora and fauna. (Of course you *could* sketch bachelor's buttons and butterflies in your backyard . . . if they'd only hold still!) Study the pictures for both unusual structures and extraordinary color combinations, which you can later incorporate into your machine stitchery. Here is a beautiful butterfly shape I'd never have thought up by myself. I traced the outline onto tissue paper and then closed the book—after all, we're not trying to copy a design line-for-line and color-for-color. These design sources should serve as take-off points for your own creativity and not further frustrate you because you can't make the machine

embroidery look exactly like the photograph you studied. (Plate 67)

Another interesting source of machine embroidery design is letter type styles, of which there are many fine books in the library. On my bookshelf I also keep the catalogs of transfer letter types that are given out free in art supply stores. If you lay a piece of transparent graph paper (also available in art supply stores) over the letter, you have an easy way to blow up the letter to any size you want—see Chapter 1. These fancy letters are quickly developed in free machine embroidery and look stunning when worked on a shiny, slightly padded surface which is quilted by your stitches. Rather than show you that straightforward approach, however,

Plate 67

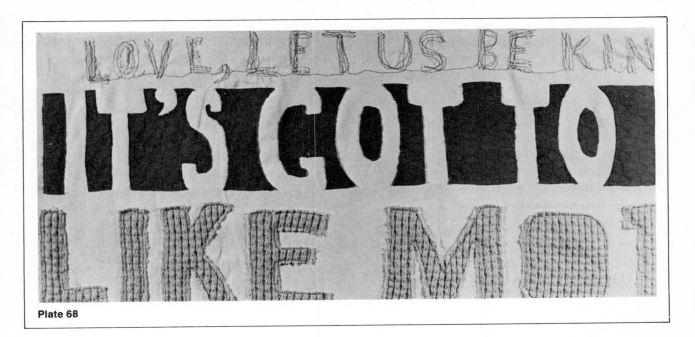

Plate 68

here is a slightly different tack. A type style was chosen and the letters traced onto tissue paper, which was then pinned to a 2″ (5cm)-wide strip of nonfraying fabric (knit) and carefully cut out with small, sharp scissors. Then all parts except the actual letters were pinned to a heavy white fabric, using the cutouts as a spacing guide, and finally were free machine stitched to the backing, using a darning foot (no hoop) with the stitch length set at 0. (Plate 68)

Gradually, after many trips to the library, you will begin to realize that ideas for machine stitchery are all around you: on greeting cards, record album covers, advertisements, magazine and book covers. Of course what makes this great wealth of material valuable or not is whether you remember all those ideas when you sit down at the machine. "I hear and I forget. I see and I remember. I do and I understand." The best way to record your ideas is to keep a file, notebook, or drawer of them.

If the idea can be cut from a magazine, do it when inspiration strikes. I like to staple these cut-outs to a sheet of 8½″ X 11″ letter-size notebook paper and immediately make notes in the margin. Many times I've enthusiastically ripped out a picture with exciting pos-

sibilities for machine embroidery, tossed it in the file, taken it out months later, and been mystified— "wonder what I saw in this old thing?" So I make notes in the margin. (Diagram 92)

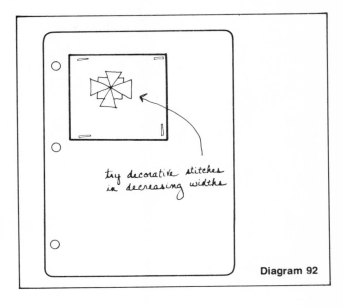

try decorative stitches in decreasing widths

Diagram 92

You can't cut up library books, of course, so it helps to have a pad of tracing paper nearby when an appealing design strikes your eye.

The reason I have suggested printed resources for inspiration, rather than first-hand observation of the world around you, is that many people do not make a habit of and are not comfortable sketching. Furthermore, it's more than a matter of not knowing how —many people are afraid to try. It doesn't help to say that drawing is merely a recording tool, just as handwriting is a recording tool. If you're afraid, you're afraid, and you have to start from that situation.

Still, there is a world of design ideas surrounding you every minute and it's a shame not to tap into something so readily available. But do you have to draw it? No, there are lots of other ways to record the design that surrounds us daily. First, though, you have to *find* the designs. It's a matter of training, just like running two miles a day is—the more you do, the easier it is, the better you get. You have to train your eye to look actively. For example, today I took my child to a nearby playground, a place we have visited hundreds of times, and I suddenly saw for the first time the pattern on the old fence next to the swing. (Plate 69)

Plate 69

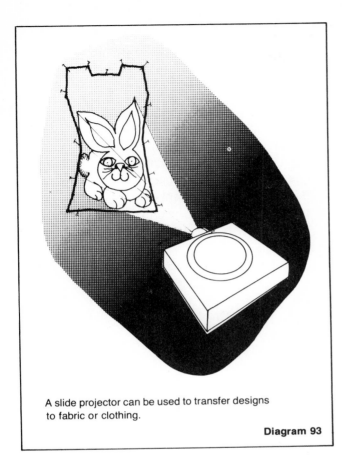

A slide projector can be used to transfer designs to fabric or clothing.

Diagram 93

The world is full of simple shapes.

Diagram 94

This would make an attractive medallion on the front of a dress. Did I draw it? No, I photographed it. The camera is a good tool to record the designs you discover in the world.

If you take slides, you can use a projector to blow up the designs you've discovered. Project the slide onto a sheet of paper on the wall, moving the projector until the outline of the picture matches the outline of the object you're planning to make, and then trace the main lines of the design. Or, trace the projected design directly on a ready-made garment. (Congratulations, you've just translated a design into a cartoon!) You can also project and trace directly onto fabric to be used in a home sewn garment. (Diagram 93)

Another way to record design without drawing is to pack up a pile of colored construction paper, some rubber cement or other glue, and scissors. Pick a place

to sit and an area to study—the houses across the street, a tree, a parking lot, a bookshelf. When you see a grouping of geometric shapes, cut one out of paper and glue it to another bigger piece of paper. Stick circles and squares, triangles and rhomboids, on top of each other. You don't have to capture every shape that's there . . . and you can capture shapes that live only in your fantasy. If you feel inspired, draw on top of your shapes, just as you would free machine stitch on top of appliquéd shapes. This cut-paper technique by the way, has been used for centuries by the Chinese as a preliminary for hand embroidery. (Diagram 94)

If you would like to improve your drawing skills— just for yourself, merely to improve your machine embroidery— the two drawing books listed in the bibliography at the end of this chapter are quite helpful.

Incidentally, that bibliography is much more than a

perfunctory offering. These are all books that I personally know to be exceedingly helpful in inspiring and developing a sense of design.

Although it's fun to follow other people's designs, finding and developing your own is thrilling. It means something to *you,* something you alone saw, recorded, and expanded into beautiful machine stitchery.

And now there's only one thing left to say . . .

ADDITIONAL IDEAS

■ You know enough now to make "December" of your fabric calendar by yourself. When you finish, wrap it up and give it to someone you love.

BOOKS THAT INFORM
AND INSPIRE

Dewey Decimal call numbers given in parentheses when known— ask your librarian for help

on learning to look:

Constance Howard, *Inspiration for Embroidery, BT* Batsford Ltd/Charles T. Branford Co., 1966, $14 (746.4).

Dona Meilach and Jay Hinz, *How to Create Your Own Designs,* Doubleday, 1975, $12 (745.4).

Wolf Strache, *Forms and Patterns in Nature,* Random House, 1973, $10, $3.95 pap.

Kjell Block Sandved, *Butterfly Magic,* Viking, 1975, $12.95 (595.7).

Peter Tompkins and Christopher Bird, *The Secret Life Of Plants,* Harper & Row, 1973, $8.95.

Richard M. Proctor, *The Principles of Pattern for Craftsmen and Designers,* Van Nostrand Reinhold, 1969, $7.95.

how to record what you see:

Kimon Nicolaides, *The Natural Way to Draw,* Houghton Mifflin Co., 1941, $4.95 pap. (741).

Philip Thiel, *Freehand Drawing: A Primer,* University of Washington Press, 1965, $4.95 (741).

what others have seen:

any of the Dover series on historical design motifs including:

George Bain, *Celtic Art: The Methods of Construction,* Dover Publications, 180 Varick St. New York, NY 10014, 1973, $4 (745.4).

Jorge Enciso, *Design Motifs of Ancient Mexico,* Dover Publications, 1953, $2.50 pap. (745.4).

Adolf Lorch, *Modern Geometric Design,* Sterling Publishing Co., 1971, $5.95 (745.4).

Max Tilke, *Costume Patterns and Designs,* Frederick A. Praeger, 1957, $49.95 (391).

Henri Romagnesi, *Exotic Mushrooms,* Sterling Publishing Co., 1971, $12.95 (589).

some artists share their vision:

Marcel Joray, editor, *Vasarely,* Griffon Neuchatel, 1965, $29.50 (704).

Ernst Haas, *The Creation,* Viking, 1971, $25 (779).

Milton Glaser, *Milton Glaser: Graphic Design,* Overlook Press, 1973, $30.

The Last Whole Earth Catalog, copyright Portola Institute, distributed by Random House, 1971, $5 (658.8).

HANDY ALL-AT-ONE-GLANCE MACHINE EMBROIDERY CHART

	chapter	stitch width	stitch length	tensions top	tensions bobbin	foot	feed dog	hoop	backing	needle	thread
automatic	7	v*	v	v	v	embroidery	in place	no	paper	v	extra-fine
beading	3	1–4	fine	tighten	loosen	embroidery	in place	no	no	10/11(70)	heavy on top
cable	6	0	0	v	bypass	darning	lower	no	no	16/18(100/110)	heavy under
circular embroidery	8	1–4	v	universal		embroidery	inplace	yes	paper	10/11(70)	extra-fine
couching-by-piercing	5	0	0	universal		darning	lower	no	interfacing	v	invisible
couching, topside	4	0	0	normal	loosen	darning	lower	no	no	v	v
couching, underside	6	0–4	10–12	loosen	bypass	presser	in place	no	no	vv	heavy under
crosshatching	2	0	0	universal		presser	in place	no	no	v	v
crosshatching, zigzag	3	1–4	10–12	universal		presser	in place	no	no	v	v
cross stitch	10	1–4	v	universal		presser	in place	no	no	v	v
cut work	9	0	0	universal		darning	lower	yes	no	v	v
detached whip stitch	5	0	0	tighten	bypass	darning	lower	yes	interfacing	v	v
edges, special	10	1–4	v	universal		embroidery	in place	yes	paper	v	v
encroaching zigzag	5	1–4	0	loosen	normal	darning	lower	yes	paper	10/11(70)	extra-fine
eyelets	8	1–4	0	universal		none	e. plate	yes	no	v	v
fagoting	7	wide	10–12	loosen	normal	embroidery	lower	no	paper	v	v
free machine embroidery	4	0	0	loosen	normal	darning	inplace	yes	v	wing	extra-fine
hemstitching	9		10–12	universal		presser	lower	no	no	10/11(70)	extra-fine
monograms	10	1–4	0	loosen	normal	darning	lower	yes	paper	v	v
needleweaving	9	1–4	0	universal		darning	lower	no	no	v	v
quilting, presser foot	2	0	10–12	loosen	loosen	presser	in place	no	paper	v	v
quilting, free	12	0	0	loosen	normal	darning	lower	no	paper	v	v
picot	8	0	10–12	universal		presser	in place	no	no	wing	extra-fine
pintucking	8	0	10–12	tighten	normal	pintuck	in place	no	no	twin	v
reverse applique	9	1–4	fine	loosen	normal	embroidery	in place	no	no	10/11(70)	extra-fine
rugmaking	7	1–4	10–12	universal		presser	in place	no	no	v	v
satin stitch	3	1–4	fine	loosen	regular	embroidery	in place	no	no	10/11(70)	extra-fine
satin stitch spots	5	1–4	0	loosen	normal	darning	lower	no	no	v	v
smocking	8	v	10–2	universal		presser	in place	no	no	v	v
stocking face dolls	9	0	0	universal		darning	lower	no	organza	10/11(70)	extra-fine
straight stitch	2	0	any	universal		presser	in place	no	no	v	v
topstitching	2	0	8–10	universal		presser	in place	no	no	v	v
trapunto	2	0	10–12	universal		presser	in place	no	organza	v	v
vari-width zigzag	3	1–4	fine	universal		embroidery	in place	no	v	v	v
whip stitch	4	0	0	tighten	bypass	presser	lower	yes	no	v	v
zigzag, open	3	1–4	10–12	universal		presser	in place	no	no	v	v
zigzag shading	5	1–4	0	loosen	tighten	darning	lower	yes	papér	10/11(70)	extra-fine

* varies

SUPPLY LIST

SEWING MACHINES

Check the yellow pages of your telephone directory or write:

Bernina Headquarters
70 North Street
Salt Lake City, Utah 84101

Brother International Corporation
680 5th Avenue
New York, NY 10019

Elna
see White Sewing Machine Company

JC Penney Co, Inc.
1301 Avenue of the Americas
New York, NY 10019

Sears' Kenmore
Sears Tower
Chicago, Ill. 60607

Morse Electro Products Corporation
101-10 Foster Avenue
Brooklyn, NY 11236

Necchi Development Corporation
63 Wall Street
New York, NY 10005

Nelco Sewing Machine Company, Inc.
164 W. 25th Street
New York, NY 10001

New Home Sewing Machine Company
171 Commerce Rd.
Carlstadt, NJ 07072

Pfaff International Corporation
373 5th Avenue
New York, NY 10016

Riccar America Company
3184 Pullman Street
Costa Mesa, CA 92626

The Singer Company
Consumer Products Division
321 First Street
Elizabeth, NJ 07207

Viking Sewing Machine Company Inc.
2300 Louisiana Avenue
Minneapolis, MN 55427

White Sewing Machine Company
11750 Berea Rd.
Cleveland, Ohio 44111

THREADS

extra-fine:

DMC 100% cotton
107 Trumbull Street
Elizabeth, NJ 07206

Bernina 100% cotton
see address under Sewing Machines

Zwicki 100% cotton
see White Sewing Machine Company address

La Paleta 100% cotton and rayon
Folklorico Yarn Company
PO Box 626
522 Ramona Street
Palo Alto, CA 94301

Riccar 100% cotton and rayon
see address under Sewing Machines

Molnlycke 100% polyester
ask your fabric store dealer

ordinary:

Belding-Corticelli 100% cotton
1430 Broadway
New York, NY 10018

JP Clark's cotton-covered polyester
430 Park Avenue
New York, NY 10022

heavy:

Molnlycke buttonhole twist
ask your fabric store dealer

crochet cotton
Coats and Clark's
430 Park Avenue
New York, NY 10022

other:

nylon invisible
Conso Products
999 Central Park Avenue
Yonkers, NY 10701

metallic (gold and silver) on spool
Talon—ask your fabric store dealer

MACHINE EMBROIDERY SUPPLIES
(hoops, threads, patterns, books, etc.)

LuRae's Creative Stitchery
PO Box 291
Bountiful, Utah 84010

Verna Holt's Machine Stitchery
700 S. Jones Blvd
Las Vegas, Nev. 89107

MISCELLANEOUS

pounce powder
Erica Wilson Needleworks
717 Madison Avenue
New York, NY 10021

transfer pencil
The Craftint Manufacturing Company
18501 Euclid Avenue
Cleveland, Ohio 44112

fabric glue
Fray Check
General Dispersions, Inc.
Bloomfield, NJ 07003

spray-on pattern positioner
3-M Company
Minneapolis, MN 55101

carpet fork and jute
Rug Crafters
3895 S. Main
Santa Ana, CA 92707

fabric paint
Versetex
Durable Arts
Box 2413
San Rafael, CA 94902

carpet fork (for adjustable hairpin lace crochet loom)
C. J. Bates & Sons, Inc.
Chester, Conn. 06412

lampshades
House of Lamps
343 Main Street
Los Altos, CA 94022

NEEDLE AND THREAD CHART

Fit the thread to the type of work or material and fit the needle to the thread

Needle	Thread	Fabrics
8/9 (60)	extra-fine	very sheer (denier,etc.)
10/11 (70)	extra-fine cotton and polyester	lightweight and transparent fabrics (net, chiffon, organza, etc.)
12 (80)	silk twist (A), ordinary cotton	lightweight cottons
14 (90)	ordinary cotton, cotton-covered polyester, silk twist (D)	wool, flannel, medium-weight cottons, jerseys
16 (100)	heavy-duty cotton	heavy coating material
18 (110)	heavy	heavy denims, etc.

INDEX